MASTER WINEMAKING

DISCOVER THE SECRETS TO MAKING PREMIUM HOMEMADE WINE IN JUST 5 SIMPLE STEPS, EVEN IF YOU'RE AN ABSOLUTE BEGINNER

TRAVIS REID

CONTENTS

APPENDICES

Master Winemaking Homemade Wine Recipe Card
(Keep track of all of your batches of wine)

This recipe card:

- Helps you keep track of each step of the winemaking process
- Provides you with a place to add your tasting notes once your wine is ready to drink

The last thing we want is for your batch of wine to be ruined because you didn't keep track of each stage of the process!

To receive your winemaking recipe card, visit the link:

www.MasterWinemaking.com/RecipeCard

WHY THIS BOOK?

We all live in a world where computers, cell phones, email, instant messaging, instant dinners, and fast food were supposed to help make us more efficient so we would have to work less.

While it's true that these "labor-saving devices" have made us more efficient, it also means that we are:

- Working faster
- Absorbing more information
- Taking on larger workloads
- Working longer hours
- Dealing with more stress

And

- Spending a lot less time doing those things we love to do!

I work in a small business environment where I experience the above daily and therefore have made an extra effort to ensure that I work smarter (not harder) so that I can enjoy my life.

One of my favorite hobbies is to make beer and wine for several reasons:

- I sit at a computer all day working in an office, so it gets me away from the computer and allows me to do something completely different
- I enjoy experimenting with different recipes and creating something unique
- I find it relaxing and an excellent stress reliever
- It is something that I enjoy discussing with other beer and winemakers as I often learn new tricks

The purpose of this book is not to convince you that you need to slow down, relax, and enjoy yourself as I'm sure you already know this. I'm also assuming that you are interested in winemaking because you had heard about it through a friend or family member and have finally decided to get involved in actually doing it! It's also possible that you've already started making a few batches of wine, are excited about what you've accomplished so far and are eager to learn more. Either way, I'm glad that you're taking the time to go through my wine-making manual as my goal is to help guide you through the wine-making process. I hope that it will, not only ensure that you make delicious wine, but that it also helps you enjoy your life that much more.

FIRST, SOME WINEMAKING HISTORY

...

DID YOU KNOW THAT WINEMAKING HAS BEEN AROUND FOR THOUSANDS OF YEARS?

It's only been in the last couple hundred years, however, that great wines were born as the science behind wine had not previously existed. When microbiologists discovered yeasts and chemists found the process of microbes consuming sugars and converting them into alcohol and gas, people were able to refine the whole process of making wine.

How old is the art of winemaking?

Archaeological evidence suggests that the earliest wine production came from the areas of Georgia near the Black Sea and Iran as early as 6,000 to 5,000 B.C. It is estimated that the first domestication of a grapevine dates back to the Bronze Age in the Near East, Sumer, and Egypt.

Wine production in Europe and Greece dates back to about 6,500 years ago. Archaeological sites in Greece have shown the world's earliest evidence of crushed grapes. In his writings, the 1st century author, naturalist, and philosopher Pliny the Elder described how the ancient Greeks used partly dehydrated gypsum before the fermentation of wine. Pliny goes on to say that a type of lime was added to the wine after fermentation to reduce acidity.

Wine played a vital role in the ancient ceremonial life of the Egyptians. It is believed that wine was introduced into Egypt by the Ancient Greeks. There is also archaeological evidence that uncovered traces of wine in China, dating from the second and first millennium BC.

Wine was a staple during the classical era of Greece and Rome. The Ancient Greeks introduced vines such as *Vitis Vinifera*, or the common grapevine, and produced wine in their colonies located in Italy, Sicily, southern France, and Spain. According to mythology, the ancient Greek God Dionysus became the symbol of wine and celebration. Homer and Aesop often referred to wine in their works.

The ancient Romans developed many wine regions in Western Europe. It was during the Roman Empire that technology vastly improved the creation and preservation of wine. It was also during this period that many grape varieties and cultivation techniques were developed, as well as the use of barrels for fermentation, aging, and transportation was also created.

DID YOU KNOW THAT WINE HAS MEDICINAL VALUE?

There is a long history of wine being used as a medical treatment as well. Often herbs and other plants were added to wine to create a tonic. One of the more unusual medicinal practices involved dissolving pearls in wine to make a health tonic. There was a famous legend about Cleopatra when she promised Marc Anthony she would "drink the value of a province" in one cup of wine. She then dissolved a pearl in the wine and drank it.

Wine was also used in the ceremonial rights of other ancient peoples. For example, agate stones were dissolved in wine to treat snakebites.

RECOMMENDED READING:

If you are interested in learning more about wine, it's many styles, how to read a commercial wine label as well as all of the work that goes into making wine at a commercial winery I highly recommend that you read *"A Taste For Wine: 20 Key Tastings To Unlock Your Personal Wine Style"* by Master Sommelier Vincent Gasnier.

You can purchase a copy on Amazon.com.

STEP ONE : TIME TO DO SOME SHOPPING!

THE FIRST STEP TO MAKING GREAT TASTING WINE IS HAVING THE RIGHT EQUIPMENT AS WELL AS UNDERSTANDING WHY YOU NEED THEM!

Lesson 1: The Big Three: Water, Sugar, and Yeast

Lesson 2: The Essentials: Sine Qua Non

Lesson 3: Choosing a Wine Kit Based on Quality, Grape & How Soon YOU Want to Enjoy It

LESSON 1: THE BIG THREE
WATER, SUGAR & YEAST

Imagine a musical stage production. You have the actors and actresses, the stagehands, the musicians, the sets, the makeup, the props, the lights, and the sound. They all work together to create magic and entertainment - you sit and are transported into another place and time.

Drinking a great wine can have that same effect based on its aroma, its color, its depth of flavor, and overall appearance.

Think about that performance. If you strip away all of the sets, music, props, and glitz, you are left with only the actors. Without the actors, the rest of the production means nothing. You can have the most exciting set in the world, and if an actress' singing turns your hair on end, that's what you will remember.

WHAT ARE THESE BIG THREE ACTORS IN WINEMAKING?

Who are the actors that are so important to the performance of wine that without them, you will taste spoiled grape juice, or worse - bad vinegar?

They are none other than *Water, Sugar,* and *Yeast*!

These three actors have to be present in any type of wine production. It doesn't matter if it is the most expensive Chardonnay or a quirky seasonal wine like pumpkin; they all contain these three actors.

Everything else you use includes the props and stage in which these actors perform. Let's look at each of these individually.

Water:

All water is not created equally!

Water is something we often take for granted every day. Unless it is dirty, most water looks the same - a clear, odorless liquid. Nobody thinks about pH or the mineral content of water - that is, except for wine and beer makers.

Water can be very different, and in a lab can be broken down into more than just oxygen and hydrogen. Water is a living substance that absorbs its environment, including chemicals, minerals, and even microscopic life. These additions to water not only affect its taste but can also alter the way it behaves during chemical reactions.

Have you ever experienced what "hard" water does when you are in the shower? Well, if you haven't had the experience, soap does not lather well as hard water contains heavy minerals that inhibit the production of bubbles and lather. Hard water can affect your wine, and as you will learn, there are additives in wine that make water more wine-friendly.

There are places in the world that wine and beer are made that can only be produced to taste a certain way due to the water used in that region. Water can make or break a wine, and so, choosing the right water is so essential.

You can try the water from your tap, but you might want to do a little research about where it comes from and how it is processed.

If you get your water from a spring or well, it can be a blessing or a curse. It will either enhance the flavor and bouquet of your wine or make it more like a "zoo in a glass."

One other thing to add regarding tap water is that some municipalities in North America add *chloramine* (in the chlorine family) to the water as it keeps it clean and resists dissipating into the atmosphere. Chloramine is very important when transporting the water over long distances. Great for cities, but it is not so suitable for winemaking.

A couple of options to consider are bottled water and spring water.

There is a wide array of bottled waters, and depending on the brand can be quite pricey. Look closely where the water comes from. It should be printed on the label, and you may be shocked to find out that a 6 dollar jug of water came from somebody's tap in New York City or Vancouver. Drinking water usually has minerals added to it to make it "taste" better. Yeast likes minerals, so not necessarily a bad thing to have them in there. Spring water has also been found to be a safe bet.

Here is the best rule of thumb overall:

If the water doesn't taste very good before you turn it into wine, it will not taste any better after it becomes wine!

Some people do not like to use distilled water as it can alter and deaden the taste of wine. Distilled water, however, is excellent when cleaning and sanitizing your equipment.

If your tap water has no real overt taste or odor, it should be fine to make wine. Do your research and experiment a little. You can use tap water to rinse and clean your equipment, but it is recommended that it is very hot or even better boiled ahead of time. When cleaning your equipment, you do want "dead" water so that you reduce contaminating it.

Sugar:

You may have noticed that I did not say fruit is needed to make wine because technically, it's the sugar that's needed.

Sugar is what is converted into alcohol (and carbon dioxide).

Some sugars ferment more easily than others do, but technically, you could make wine from about any sugar. After all, people have made wine using rhubarb, dandelions, apples, raspberries, Ribena, and even prawns.

Different foods contain different amounts of sugar, so sugar is sometimes added to the wine to help the fermentation process. Without sugar, you would essentially have water and yeast, with no fermentation "magic."

Yeast:

Yeast consists of microscopic creatures who are responsible for the magic that makes it all happen.

They are found in every fermented product: beer, wine, yogurt, bread, tofu, and even old fashion soft drinks. They are a hardy creature who can live in a freeze-dried state until they are reconstituted by water.

They live and exist to do two things - eat sugar and procreate.

When they eat their fill of sugar, they split, procreate, and die.

When the yeast eats the sugar, they excrete two things - gas and alcohol. The gas is carbon dioxide, and when you make your first batch, you will understand this process more clearly.

NOTE: You can't just use any yeast from your kitchen cabinet or pantry!

I heard a story about a person who made batch after batch of lousy wine, and he couldn't figure out what was happening. After all, he had the big three - water, sugar, and yeast. He had all the right equipment that he scrubbed after every use.

So why was his wine not fit for a dog?

The reason it was awful was that he wasn't making wine - he was making liquid bread as he was using baker's yeast!

I'll assure you that it will turn the sugars in your wine into alcohol, but part of the taste of wine is the yeast. Yes, as you take a sip of that fruity Pinot Grigio, you are also consuming the remnants of dead yeast, but these add to the flavor and complexity of your wine.

In the old days, wine was made by crushing grapes with feet. Depending on your "vintage" you potentially have seen that famous episode of "I Love Lucy" where everyone jumped into big vats of grapes and stomped the grapes until it was a mass of juice, stems, seeds, and whatever was on your feet to start with.

They put the juice into barrels, and the miracle happened - the grape juice turned into wine.

How did this happen? Where did the yeast come from? The answer is the grape skins. Yeast resides on the outside of grapes - wild yeast is everywhere.

The wine yeasts that you can buy today are grown in labs!

These yeasts are harvested from wine and cultured. In some cases, they're placed in vials in a nutrient-rich liquid or are freeze-dried and put into packets. They vary in price, but you can get away with decent wine yeast for about $1 but can spend as much as $10 for a higher quality liquid yeast.

Here are some links to some excellent resources if you'd like to learn more about yeast:

WineMaker Magazines Yeast Strain Chart

- www.winemakermag.com/referenceguide/yeaststrainschart/

"Lallemand (Lalvin)" Brand Yeast

- www.lallemandwine.com

"White Labs" Brand Yeast

- www.whitelabs.com

"Wyeast" (pure liquid yeast)

- www.wyeastlab.com/hw_products.cfm

TYPES OF FERMENTATION:

Since liquid needs a container, the first piece of equipment that you will need is the bucket

(aka "the Primary").

I will concede that you do not need a bucket as wine has been made in prison toilets for years. Not that I would want to drink any - but technically any liquid containing vessel could produce a wine like substance. I have personally used a sanitized green garbage can to make wine!

Since you want to make wine to impress your friends and not make something that will cause them to run to the nearest Emergency room, we will talk about your options for containers.

You must make an important choice first – open fermentation or closed fermentation.

Open Fermentation:

Open fermentation is a drawback from the old way to make wine - a large open vessel is where juice "magically" turned into wine.

I say "magically" because our ancestors knew that if you left juice under certain conditions, it turned into wine. I am not quite sure that they knew exactly how the wine created itself and the fact that they had many great festivals to the gods and goddesses to help ensure a great batch of wine occurred is proof of this.

You can use a plastic or a glass container, and in some situations, you can also use a ceramic vessel; however, these are usually very heavy and fragile. If you choose plastic, it must be food grade (i.e., it is approved for use with food products). If you do not use food grade plastic, you risk the plastic leeching into your wine and creating off-flavors and smells. You can purchase food-grade plastic containers at hardware stores, beer and wine stores, online sources, and even restaurant supply outlets. The standard vessel looks like a large white plastic pickle container used in restaurants.

If you choose to use an open container system to make wine, it is suggested that you cover it with a plastic bag to keep dust and critters out of your wine - especially fruit flies who love open containers of fruit juice.

If you're adventurous, you can try to use the wild yeasts from the air to ferment your wine, and this works better if you're using freshly pressed fruit juice.

The problem with an open container system is contamination. Remember, this is a book on wine, not vinegar. Bacteria and harmful yeasts are in the air. If you do not start your batch with good wine-making yeast, then harmful yeasts and bacteria can take over and spoil your wine very quickly.

The most definite sign that you are creating vinegar is what they call the "Mother."

The "Mother" is a slimy white thing that grows on top of or inside the liquid in your vessel. If this occurs, not only do I suggest dumping your wine, but I would also recommend you get rid of your vessel as the bacteria that makes vinegar often hides in the vessel and will continue to ruin your future batches.

Closed Fermentation:

Closed fermentation is not too different from the open fermentation system. It essentially requires one more item - a lid.

The lid sometimes has a rubber ring on its underside, which provides for a good tight seal. Some lids that you buy from wine supply stores already have a hole drilled, or they have a hole drilling service. You want that hole.

A fermentation lock (aka "airlock") needs to be purchased as well as it allows gas to be released but does not allow bad things into the vessel.

It does this by adding a water barrier. Gas bubbles up through the water barrier but does not easily allow bacteria back through it. You do need to change the water in the fermentation lock once every couple of days, and it is recommended that you use sanitized water (we will discuss sanitizers in a later Lesson). If you do not use a sanitizer, you should at least boil and distill the water.

The lid is snapped on tight, and the fermentation lock is inserted into the drilled hole. Imagine you are holding a water balloon that is ¾ quarters full of water. Now imagine adding air to the balloon. Very soon, you will be all wet! A fermentation vessel would do the same without the fermentation lock.

In a closed system, a glass vessel called a carboy can be used. A carboy is usually used as a secondary fermentation container, but if you are limited on funds, it can be used as a primary fermentation vessel as well.

Some batches you make may be small, especially when you are using fresh fruit from the local market. In this case, you would not use a six-gallon bucket to make a gallon of wine. You would choose a 1.5-gallon carboy instead. If you leave too much room in a fermentation vessel, you risk contaminating your wine.

When wine is fermenting, it releases nitrogen, which creates a gas barrier above the wine that insulates it from contamination. If your space is too large, the nitrogen barrier will not be dense enough to protect your wine.

A carboy has a neck and an opening at the top. A rubber cork, called a "bung," is stuck in this opening.

When purchasing a bung, there are two essential things you must know:

1. They come in different sizes. Make sure the bung fits the size of the carboy you are using. You can ask any wine supplier for assistance.
2. Make sure the bung has a hole drilled in it so that you can add a fermentation lock to it

The same kind of fermentation lock can be used in top of the bung that you use for a plastic bucket lid. Glass carboys come in different sizes from less than a gallon to 20-gallon sizes. If you can only choose one, try to get something between a 5 and 6-gallon size as it is the most versatile size and will work well with any wine kit or wine recipe.

LESSON 2: THE ESSENTIALS

SINE QUA NON

Sine Qua Non (definition): Without which, not; an indispensable condition.

There are certain items that you will need to make great wine. These are the *"Sine Qua Non"* of home winemaking. Once you have gathered these items, you will be ready to make your first batch of wine.

Here is a list of what you'll need:

1. Primary fermenter (30 liters or 8 US gallons)
2. Secondary fermenter (carboy – 23 liters or 6 gallons)
3. Airlock & bung
4. Sanitizer (B-Brite, C-Brite or potassium metabisulfite)
5. Brushes (bottle brush and carboy brush)
6. Spoon

7. Tubing

8. Bottles

9. Bottle filler

10. Corks

11. Corker (hand corker or floor corker)

12. Wine thief

13. Hydrometer

14. Floating thermometer

15. Auto Siphon

16. Carboy handle

SANITIZER:

When you cook in the kitchen, do you use dirty pots or put food down on a dirty countertop? Apart from being gross, you increase the likelihood of becoming sick or, at the very least, adding something to your dish that you do not want—the same thing with winemaking. Make sure you clean the area that you will be making your wine in (including cleaning the floors and countertops) as well as sanitize every piece of equipment you will be using.

There are different types of sanitizers available. *B-Brite* and *C-Brite* are a couple of the more popular types of sanitizer and come in powder form. They are mixed in hot water, and a few spoonfuls can make about a gallon of sanitizer. It kills harmful bacteria but is safe enough to drink; therefore, you do not have to rinse after using it. You sanitize, let the equipment dry, and then use it. It has an iodine base, which is what kills the bacteria. It is recommended that you use this type of product because it does not leave any after taste or residue that can ruin your wine.

Another mainstream sanitizer is *potassium metabisulfite.* It is used in the wine as a sterilizer and a stabilizer, as well as a cleaner for equipment.

Using it is simple:

If your equipment is free of debris:

- Create a solution of potassium metabisulfite by dissolving 50g (about eight teaspoons) of the sulfite crystals, which are available at all wine equipment stores into 4L of cold water.
- You can clean your equipment by either pouring the solution over the equipment, by using a cloth to spread the solution over the item to be cleaned or (my personal favorite) you can use a spray bottle to spray your equipment down as well. Be sure to thoroughly rinse the equipment with warm water once it has been sanitized. Keep the remaining solution in a sealed container – can be used for up to 2 months.
- **HINT** - This solution has a pungent smell, so be sure to clean your equipment with the solution in a well-ventilated area.

If your equipment is stained and/or has debris:

- If your equipment has stains or smells from the previous wine and/or has debris, consider using a detergent such as "*Sani-Brew,*" which is also available at most winemaking equipment stores. Dissolve 3.5 g per L of cold water to make a sanitizing solution. Allow equipment to soak for at least 20 minutes. Rinse thoroughly with hot water. Soak heavily stained equipment for up to 48 hours.

MANY people I know are sulfite-sensitive, and so the addition of this chemical to wine can lead to severe allergic reactions, so ensure that you thoroughly rinse your equipment before you use it to make wine.

If you use a chlorine-based product, your wine will taste like chlorine unless you rinse thoroughly.

Also, if you use steel, it can turn your wine black. It can also cause adverse reactions with rubber, plastic, and other chemicals used in winemaking. If you use dish soap to clean your winemaking equipment, you will have soapy wine. Soap creates a residue on equipment that is absorbed when water comes in contact with it.

What do you use sanitizer on? EVERYTHING! You can never over clean anything, but you can certainly under clean equipment. Before doing anything with your equipment, sanitize it. Even if you sanitized a piece of equipment before storing it, you must sanitize it again before you use it.

BRUSHES:

Two different brushes are recommended when beginning winemaking, the *carboy brush,* and the *bottle brush*.

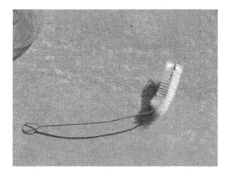

Carboy Brush

Bottle Brush

Both brushes should be sanitized every time they are used. The brushes are used to loosen debris from the inside of the wine bottles and the carboy.

The *carboy brush* is broad and slightly bent. This bend enables you to clean the top of the carboy.

The *bottle brush* is small and fits into most types of bottles.

THE SPOON:

Some would argue whether this is an essential item or not.

I think that using the same spoon you mixed last

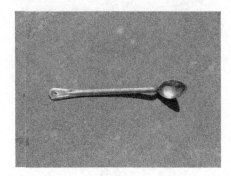

night's chili is not the best spoon to use. The best choices for materials for a "wine spoon" are food-grade plastic and stainless steel. Wood is too porous, and little critters can set up lovely little homes in the pores and ruin your wine.

Make sure the handle is long enough to reach down into your fermentation vessel. You do not want to have to reach into the bucket to stir your wine, or to retrieve a wayward spoon.

Like every other item you use in winemaking, your spoon has a singular mission - winemaking. Make sure that you clean and sanitize your spoon each time that you use it. If you lay it down between uses, make sure you sanitize it again before sticking it back into the wine. To make sure no one makes a mistake and cleans the bottom of the koi pond with it, hang a tag, or put a label on the spoon that reads,

"For wine use only. Any other use is punishable by banning the user from the next home wine tasting".

TUBING:

If you buy your winemaking equipment as a kit, they will sometimes forget to add this item. The tubing is used to transport (rack) wine between vessels. Tubing is also essential when it comes time to fill your bottles with wine. There are certain items that you will buy that over time you will need to replace. Tubing is one of those items, as cleaning the tubing is difficult. Even if you do, over time, it can wear down and harden. The good news is that tubing is cheap. Tubing is one of those items you can buy by the yard or meter at your local hardware store. You need to make sure that you buy the right diameter. Bring the items such as your bottle filler and your spigot from your primary fermenter with you when purchasing tubing. It is a good idea to buy extra in case you need to switch out your tubing.

There are little bottle brushes that are attached to monofilament string that you can pull through your tubing to make sure it is clean. If you can't find them at a wine equipment supply store, then make a trip to your nearest aquarium store as they'll have them for cleaning the fish tank filters. The best thing to do when using tubing is to soak it in sanitizer before you use it.

HERE IS WHAT I DO WHENEVER I AM READY TO BEGIN A WINEMAKING SESSION:

- I fill a fermentation bucket with hot water and sanitizer.
- I dump all of my items I am going to use during the winemaking session into the bucket.
- I let the items soak for 30 minutes.
- Make sure you rinse items with hot water to clean off any debris before you put them into the sanitizing bucket.
- Make sure your tubing is clean before storing it because wine and debris can solidify in the tubing, and then it will be impossible to clean.

BOTTLE FILLER:

*This item **is essential**.*

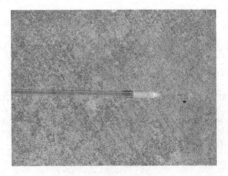

You could fill bottles by controlling the spigot, but I don't recommend it unless you enjoy sticky floors. The bottle filler is a long hard plastic tube with a spring mechanism on the tip of it. When you press the tip down on the bottom of a bottle, it allows the wine to fill the bottle. When you release pressure on the filler, it stops the flow.

There is another function of the filler that not many people are aware of. Suppose you pick up a bottle of commercial wine, you will notice that the wine is not filled to the cork, and there is some space in the bottle. This space allows gas that is trapped in the wine somewhere to go. Without this space, you will create a costly pop gun. The gas will push your cork right out of the bottle. There is nothing quite as exciting as hearing a weird popping sound and entering the room where you were storing your wine, only to find that you have redecorated your ceiling in a beautiful wine color. "Old Faithful" has nothing on exploding bottles of wine.

The bottle filler displaces enough room that when you withdraw it from the bottle, it leaves enough headroom in the bottle to help prevent wine showers in your house. You will learn later on that if your wine is not finished fermenting before you transfer it to your bottles, that you will still have the problem of exploding wine. For now, just spend that $20.00 or less on a bottle filler.

BOTTLES:

If there is an expense in home winemaking, it's the bottles.

If you buy a ready-made winemaking kit from a specialty store, I will bet it doesn't include the three cases of bottles you will need once your wine is ready.

If you don't have bottles ready, I would not recommend starting a batch of wine unless you intend to drink it right from the carboy. That might sound strange, but wine used to be drunk that way.

I have seen large glass vessels that had a tap on the bottom. Oil was poured on top of the wine. The oil floats on the wine, and so does not affect the taste (that much), and it creates a barrier from harmful bacteria or wild yeasts from attacking your wine. I, therefore, recommend using wine bottles.

You can buy all sizes, colors, and styles of bottles. Any will work for wine, but make sure you do some simple wine calculations to determine how much wine you are making and how many bottles you will need. FYI - A typical wine kit will produce 29-30 750 ml bottles of wine.

WARNING! There is an exception to the "use any bottle" rule. If you intend to make champagne, you MUST buy champagne bottles. Champagne has carbon dioxide gas trapped in it and creates an enormous amount of pressure on the bottle.

Also, you are wiring down the cork, so it will not be pushed out of the bottle. Champagne bottles have thicker walls that can withstand these high pressures. If you use regular bottles, you will create glass shard bombs that WILL do damage and CAN hurt you. I do not recommend making champagne until you have mastered making other wines first.

Wine bottles can be very pricey, but here is where your friends come in. You ask them to save their empty bottles. You can wash, sterilize, and reuse wine bottles. I always tell my friends that they can have a bottle of my wine as long as they either donate an empty bottle or two or bring back the bottle when they are done. Most wine bottles can be reused. The exception is a bottle with a screw top; it is almost impossible to get a cork in them.

Other suggestions on where you can source wine bottles:

- *From your local bottle depot or wherever you recycle your wine bottles.* In our community, you can purchase empty wine bottles for as little as $2 per dozen. The main drawback here is that you must ensure that the inside of the bottles are free of debris (including mold, cigarette butts, etc.) and are both clean and sanitized.

- *Make friends with the "barkeep" at your local bar or pub*. Ask them to save their wine bottles for you and that you will pick them up.

Getting wine labels off the bottles can be tricky!

Some are easy, and some are put on with industrial strength glue. The easiest way to get them off the bottle is to soak them in hot water for a couple of hours and then peel the label off. If they don't come off quickly, you can use a scouring pad and try to get them off.

I've found using a razor blade attached to a handle works well – you can find them at your local hardware store as they sell them to clean the gunk off of windows. If this is too frustrating, then just leave the label on the bottle.

Now, of course, if all of this sounds like more work then you are interested in then by all means head down to your local winemaking supply store (or even your local supermarket) and buy brand new bottles. They'll cost you around $1 a bottle.

CORKS:

You might have bottles now, but how do you close them? Corks, of course!

Corks are one of the things you need to buy and have on hand. You cannot recycle corks. You could make a log cabin or trivets made of used corks, but once they are used, they cannot be used in a bottle again.

Corks are running out because the trees that they are harvested from are not being replaced quickly enough. Also, you sometimes risk contamination with corks.

There's also a *"cork taint"* caused by a chemical called TCA (2,4,6-trichloroanisole), which is a fungus-created compound that invades cork fiber and can ruin the taste and aroma of the wine.

You can buy synthetic corks, but these are not recommended for aging a wine because they are not porous and do not allow a bottle of wine to "breathe." There is, unfortunately, no way to tell if a cork is bad or not until you use it. Some people soak their corks in sanitizer before they use them, which is fine, but corks can swell, making it difficult to insert them into the bottle.

Corks come in different diameters and grades

The larger they are, the better the seal, but it also makes it more challenging to insert, especially if you are using a hand corker. The grade of cork has to do with how they are made. Many of the cheaper corks are composite (aka "pressed" or agglomerated) corks that are stuck together with glue and are typically used with wines that you don't plan on aging past three years.

CORKER:

Many wine equipment kits come with this strange looking device called a *corker*.

You open it, drop a cork into it, then squeeze it back together and hold it over the top of the neck of the bottle.

You then use the plunger to insert the cork into the bottle. It takes hand strength, upper body strength, and dexterity to get the cork into the bottle. The cork should be inserted into the neck with nothing sticking over the top.

The higher-grade corks are a little softer than the composite ones and are easier to get into the bottle. We will talk about upgrading equipment in a lesson further on. I would recommend that a floor corker is on your birthday gift list. It will make life much easier for you.

NOTE: You can only use hand corkers for agglomerated corks and therefore must use a floor corker with synthetic and natural corks

WINE THIEF:

In my humble opinion using a wine thief is an essential item as this is by far the easiest way to remove a sample of the wine must from either your primary or secondary.

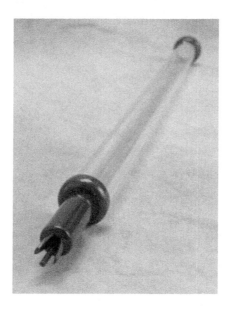

Like the bottle filler, the wine thief has a valve at the end that opens when you push it into a liquid then closes when you pull the wine thief up. There are a couple of types of wine thiefs that you can purchase. The one that I like to use has an open end at the top, which is nice because you can insert your hydrometer into it and makes testing your *specific gravity* that much easier.

HYDROMETER:

Water has a specific density or gravity. Other liquids have either a greater or a lesser density than water. The density has to do with particles suspended in the liquid. Alcohol has a lesser density than water does.

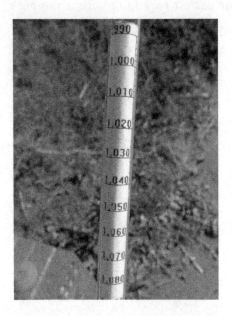

A hydrometer is an instrument that tests the density of a liquid relative to the density of water. It will determine the *specific gravity (S.G.)* of the liquid and is the most important indicator of which stage your wine is at.

The hydrometer is an enclosed glass tube that has mercury in the bottom as a weight. Materials such as sugar make the water denser and hence push the hydrometer higher in the water resulting in a lower reading.

You check this reading when you first prepare your wine before it begins to ferment. Through the process of fermentation, this sugar is transformed into alcohol. Alcohol weighs less than water. When fermentation ends, the hydrometer will be lower in the wine and, therefore, will have a higher reading.

You read the numbers from a paper scale that is inside the glass tube. You read the number that is immediately below the meniscus (curve) of the surface of the wine.

To take a *specific gravity* reading using your hydrometer, do the following:

1. Sanitize a *wine thief* and your *hydrometer.*
2. Insert the *hydrometer* into the *wine thief.*
3. Remove the airlock and bung from either your carboy or primary and insert the *wine thief* into the wine must allowing the wine to fill the *wine thief* so that the *hydrometer* floats freely.
4. Remove the *wine thief* from the primary or secondary and place the airlock back onto the neck or hole. *Hint:* You might want to place your free hand under the *wine thief* as it tends to leak a bit at the bottom.
5. Swirl the liquid in the *wine thief* so that you remove any bubbles trapped in the liquid so that you can get an accurate reading.
6. Check the *specific gravity* reading by looking at the number under the meniscus (curve) at the top of the liquid. Match this reading to the reading the instructions suggest you should have at that stage.

Note: Most wine kits will start with an S.G. reading in the 1.070 to 1.090 range (depending on the amount of sugar in your juice) and will then decrease moving close to the 1.010 mark as the yeast begins turning the sugar into alcohol. Remember, alcohol is less dense than water, which is why the S.G. reading lowers, the more prolonged the fermentation process continues.

To calculate the approximate value of the alcohol content in your wine, use the following formula:

$$\text{Approximate Alcohol Content (\%)} = \frac{\text{Starting S.G.- Ending S.G.}}{0.0074}$$

For example:

Starting SG = 1.090
Ending SG = 0.995

$$\% \text{ Alcohol} = \frac{1.090 - 0.995}{0.0074} = \frac{0.095}{0.0074} = 12.84$$

> You can, therefore, say that the approximate alcohol content of this batch of wine is 12.84%

Note: This method assumes that the difference in specific gravity is solely due to the conversion of sugar into alcohol

When you buy wine kits or read wine recipes, you will notice two readings:

1. Starting Gravity (S.G.) - this is the starting or original gravity
2. Overall Gravity (O.G.) - this is the final gravity.

O.G. is an excellent guide to know when your wine is done. If your O.G. is close to the number listed, you know that your wine is about finished fermenting. You can test it daily until the number stops changing, and this is a good indication that your wine is ready for bottling. If you bottle your wine too soon, you may want to refer to the prior section about exploding bottles.

Hydrometers usually come as "triple" hydrometers meaning that it has three different scales on them. Make sure you are reading the right scale, as the other two are usually used for beer making.

FLOATING THERMOMETER:

An essential condition for wine is temperature. There are two main times that you will want to know the temperature of your wine:

1. **When you are testing your wine with a hydrometer** - If your wine is not about room temperature, your hydrometer reading may not be accurate. You will need to either change the temperature of the wine or adjust your reading number. It is recommended that you change the temperature as making adjusted calculations can be very difficult.

2. **Fermentation requires a specific temperature (18 – 24 C) to occur** - Yeast is funny that way. Yeast likes it slightly warmer than room temperature to be happy and procreating. If it is too hot, they will die. If it is too cold, the yeast will go dormant, and you will have a condition referred to as "stuck fermentation." It means that the yeast has stopped fermenting too early in the process. Usually, raising the temperature of the vessel by a few degrees can get the yeast going again. In other situations, new inoculation of yeast may be required.

The thermometers used for winemaking are handy because they float. I still recommend you attach a monofilament string to them, as they do not always float up and down sometimes they lay horizontally and you will need the string to pull it out of the wine, instead of your fingers.

ALWAYS remember to sanitize your thermometer every time you use it.

HINT: If temperature control in your winemaking area is an issue, consider using a "Brew Belt." It's a rubber belt that attaches around your primary bucket and then is plugged into your electrical socket and keeps your wine must at a consistent 22 C (72 F). Note that you can only use this on the primary (as your secondary is made out of glass and will potentially crack if you expose it to heat). The brew belt is only needed during the first three days of the fermentation process, as this is when most of the fermentation will occur.

AUTO SIPHON:

Have you ever had to draw gasoline from your car and started the flow by sucking on one end of the tube?

Remember the awful taste in your mouth and the mess it created? Same thing in winemaking if you rely solely on using the tubing you purchased.

The auto-siphon makes racking (transferring) your wine must from one container to the other easy. Something you should consider getting!

CARBOY HANDLE:

If you've ever had to try lifting, moving, or carrying a carboy full of wine, you'll know that it's pretty heavy!

Getting a handle for your carboy is going to make moving your carboy so much easier and will undoubtedly save you from hurting your back!

LESSON 3: CHOOSING A WINE KIT

BASED ON QUALITY, GRAPE & HOW SOON YOU'D LIKE TO TRY IT!

By now you should have all of the necessary, essential equipment, and you are undoubtedly itching to make that first batch of wine, so now is the time to buy a wine kit! Wine kits have all of the ingredients and step-by-step instructions to make some of the best wine you have ever experienced.

There are different levels of wine kits. You can usually guess by the price of a kit, whether it is a beginner/intermediate wine kit or if it is advanced. Remember, all wine is basically the same and only needs the big three (water, yeast, and sugar).

So what's the difference? The grapes essentially.

The higher the quality grape and the more significant amount of juice, the more it costs. Also, higher-end wine kits usually recommend that you age them longer. Due to the grape being of superior quality, they tend to be able to age better, and they have the complexity to become an outstanding fine wine.

Some of the higher-end kits also include some additional ingredients. We will discuss high-end wine kits in Lesson 5.

SO HOW DO YOU CHOOSE THE RIGHT KIT?

1. First, pick a type of wine you like. There are so many different types of wines to choose from, so it's best to choose something that you like. Could be a Chardonnay, a Piesporter, a Riesling, a Cabernet or a Merlot.

2. Do your research. Look online and see what the reviews of a particular wine kit and a wine kit manufacturer are. Magazines such as *"Winemaker Magazine"* are a great place to look.

If you have a wine supply shop nearby, ask the owner what kind of kit they recommend. Call them on the phone as most wine shop owners LOVE to talk about wine. They can make some recommendations of what would be an excellent kit to start with, and they can recommend other kits later on as you progress.

Some wine kit makers that you should consider looking at include:

- Vine Co - www.VineCoWine.com
- Mosti Mondiale - www.MostiMondiale.com
- Wine Experts – www.Winexpert.com
- RJ Spagnols – www.RJSpagnols.com

3. Look for kits that state that you can have wine in 28 days. These are simple wines that do not require aging and can be found in most supermarkets. These are an excellent choice for your first wine.

In the next lesson, we will tear the top off a typical wine kit, see what is inside, and we will make your first wine together.

STEP TWO: LET'S MAKE WINE!

YOU HAVE THE EQUIPMENT – NOW WHAT?

LESSON 4: 9 COMMON SENSE TIPS THAT'LL MAKE WINEMAKING A WHOLE LOT EASIER!

I've heard that there are a couple of ways to go about getting the job done. Both may get you the results you want. One way is the easy way; the other is the hard way. Which will you choose? I recommend the easy way. This book is packed with tips and suggestions of winemakers who were once like you. You may want to take the time and learn from our mistakes. It can save you time, money, and, indeed, heartache.

In this lesson, I am offering you some tips that will make your winemaking experience easier from the start.

1. Find the best place to make and store your wine - this may be two different places. You need to make wine in a place with the following considerations:

- Do you have enough room to work and store your wine?

- Is there a water source nearby?
- Can you make a mess? (You will make one)
- Is it away from small children and animals? Remember, you will have deep buckets of liquid, and this can be a drowning hazard
- Is it in the way? Don't pick an area where there is a lot of traffic

Some areas that can work well are bathrooms, utility rooms (where the washer and dryer are located), utility buildings, and garages. As far as where you store the bucket to ferment, it should be warm and temperature controlled. When you need to age or store the wine, it should be a cool, dark place.

2. Have all of your supplies together. Nothing can break your concentration if you have to hunt down a piece of equipment that is lost. Make sure you have gathered everything you need and that everything has been sanitized.

3. Give yourself enough time. If you have to rush a step because you promised to go out to dinner, you could ruin your wine. Look at the directions and give yourself plenty of time to set up, work, and clean up. If you leave stuff sitting around and dirty, you are begging for contamination.

4. Have a bucket of sanitizer ready as you need to place items into it. As you use an item, drop it into the bucket. That way, if you need to use it later, it will be ready to go. **Have a chair or a**

stool handy. Some of this can be back-breaking work. It is nice to be able to sit and rest between steps.

5. Have a stool, counter, or table to set items on. It is essential when you have to transfer liquid from one container to another. Gravity does not work uphill. One container has to be higher than the other. The higher it is, the faster the liquid will move. If you feel like you could use some extra counter space, then a suggestion would be to go down to your local Costco or office supply center and purchase one of those folding tables with metal legs and a durable plastic tabletop. They are relatively inexpensive and add quick and easy counter space. I purchased one from Costco for around $40, and it works well.

6. When the instructions say, *stir*, make sure you do it! One thing that you will note in the instructions that come with your wine kit is that it will ask you to "stir vigorously" at various points throughout the process. It is usually at the beginning so that you mix the bentonite and grape concentrate with the water, and at the end of the process to remove excess carbon dioxide (also known as "degassing")

HINT: Use a "Fizzex" bit for your drill as it will stir the wine must without disturbing the surface (so you won't introduce as much oxygen), and it will be much easier on the arm. They are available at most winemaking stores for around $24.95.

7. Clean up your mess. I mentioned this earlier. You need to clean the area after you use it and make sure everything you used is clean and sanitized for the next use. Your family will thank you. Make sure you have a closet or area to store your equipment in.

8. Have a glass of wine ready. When you are done or even between steps, it is always nice to have a glass of wine. It relaxes you and inspires you to make more. Kick back and remember - this is a hobby, not a job!

9. The two ultimate determining success factors for your wine would be both *"time"* **and** *"patience."* Did you know that your average wine kit is typically ready to bottle in 28 to 45 days? It doesn't necessarily mean that they are ready to drink, though, as most kits require some form of aging anywhere from 3 months to a year or more depending on the kit.

LESSON 5: WHAT'S ALL THIS STUFF?

Hopefully by now you have purchased your first wine kit, and it may look something like this:

WHAT'S ALL THAT STUFF INSIDE?

Let's go through your kit and explain each part. Then you will use these items as we go step by step through the winemaking process.

The kit that is used in this lesson may be different than yours; however, the steps are pretty much the same for each kit. Make sure you READ and RE-READ the instructions included in the kit. The directions were created by people who have used the particular kit you are attempting many times before they put it on the market. Some of the directions may seem odd, but trust me, if you try to improvise right from the starting block, you could ruin your wine quite quickly.

Let's have a look at what you should have in front of you:

Juice bag:

This is the grape juice. The grapes have already been pressed, and the juice is in concentrate form. It is concentrated so that it will be easier to package. If there are multiple bags (especially if your kit is in a bucket), it means the water and grape juice has already been combined, and therefore no additional water needs to be added. Your wine kit will tell you if you need to add water.

Some bags may have a vintage date on them. This date represents the year the grapes were picked and pressed.

Yeast packet:

It is the type of yeast that best fits the style of wine that you have chosen.

Look carefully at the date on the yeast packet. If it is old, then consider purchasing another yeast packet of the same kind of yeast – don't worry as yeast packets as shown on the left are cheap. If the yeast packet that came in your kit is old, the yeast may not ferment right, and you may experience what is called a "stuck" fermentation, which we discussed earlier on.

HINT: If "stuck fermentation occurs," extract some of the must (the must is what the wine is called when it is fermenting). Take about a cup of must and add some fresh yeast to it and mix it at room temperature. Allow it to sit covered for about 15 minutes. Then add the must and yeast back to your wine, which should jump-start your fermentation again.

* * *

Bentonite:

Bentonite is a naturally occurring gray clay that contains sodium, calcium, magnesium, and iron. It helps clear the wine and speeds up the onset of fermentation. It is used as a clarifier because it has an ion charge that attracts particles in the wine must. It then drags these to the bottom of the must. When you *rack* (remove clear wine from the sludge on the bottom), the lees (the sludge) are left behind.

Potassium Metabisulfite:

Potassium metabisulfite is added to wine to inhibit bacteria and yeast growth, as well as to slow down oxidation. It may leave an unpleasant aftertaste in wine if you use too much.

This chemical is also used in a water solution as an antiseptic rinse to sanitize equipment. It is identical to, but better than, Sodium Metabisulfite, because it does not add sodium to one's diet. It may come in the form of Campden tablets, which are crushed and added to the wine must, especially when you make wine out of fresh fruit.

Sorbate (Potassium Sorbate):

Potassium sorbate is used to slow down yeast growth and inhibit fermentation, thus "stabilizing" your wine before bottling.

It is used later on in the process, so make sure you put it in a safe place.

Isinglass:

Isinglass is a pure form of gelatin and comes from the air bladder of certain fish, usually the sturgeon.

It's used as a fining agent to help clarify (clear) your wine when bottling it.

Extra Juice (aka "F-Pack" or "Süsse-Reserve"):

In the kit I am using as a demonstration, there is another smaller juice packet.

It is a different fruit juice that adds a specific flavor to the wine (like apple, mango, or kiwi). This juice is added at the end and is NOT fermented. That is why it is in a separate bag.

Here's a list of other possible ingredients in your kit and an explanation of them:

Acid Blend - This compound is used to raise the acidity of the wine must, thus increasing tartness. It is comprised of equal amounts of malic, tartaric, and citric acid. It is usually used when creating a wine that is not in a kit, as the acid blend is usually already added to your juice concentrate.

Ascorbic Acid - This reduces oxidation (think *rust*) in bottled wine when added just before bottling.

Bocksin - This solution of silicium dioxide removes H2S (hydrogen sulfide) odors and related off-flavors in wine. It will remove the smell of rotten eggs. It must be added immediately to be effective. Sometimes there is nothing to do but dump the wine if bocksin does not work.

Calcium Carbonate - Calcium Carbonate lowers the acidity of your wine. It is the opposite of the acid blend. Again, this is usually for recipe wines rather than kit wines. Calcium carbonate is often used in place of adding water to achieve a more basic wine, since adding water will dilute your wine.

Grape Tannin - This is a chemical that is found in many white wine kits because it is usually already in the red wine juice kits and is naturally found in the skins and stems of grapes. It adds astringency or zest to wine. It is also used in the clearing process.

Lysozyme – A Lysozyme solution is used in wine to hinder or prevent malolactic fermentation. It controls lactic acid bacteria and is made from an enzyme that naturally occurs in egg whites. I have heard that you can use egg whites as a clarifier in secondary fermentation. Make sure you have only egg whites as the yolk may not combine well and could spoil your wine.

Oak Chips – Some kits include oak shavings or chips (or a combination of the two) to add an oaky flavor to your wine. They are typically added right at the beginning of the winemaking process.

Pectic Enzyme - Pectic enzyme increases juice yields from fruits by breaking down cellular structures. It also acts as a clarifier and is used to clear hazes caused by residual pectins. It is usually used in stone fruit wines (plums, peaches). These fruits have high levels of pectin and can be very hazy and may oxidize if not cleared.

Sparkalloid - Sparkalloid is used as a fining agent and is usually a powder, although it can come in liquid form as well.

Some other items I've seen added to wine kits include raisins and grape skins. Both helped enhance the flavor of the style of wine I was making.

LESSON 6: STEREO INSTRUCTIONS

Have you ever bought a stereo or other "do it yourself" projects and read the instructions, after which you said "Huh?" The instructions in wine kits can be a little unclear at times. Here is the primary line up of instructions for any wine:

NOTE: I've put together a *Winemaking Recipe Card* for you so that you can easily keep track of all of your batches of wine. A copy is included in *Appendix 2,* and additional copies can be downloaded for FREE by going to www.MasterWinemaking.com/RecipeCard

PREPARATION:

1. Get your gear together and clean it. You will need:

- Wine Kit

- Spoon
- Primary Fermenter
- Bung and Airlock
- Clean Water
- Sanitizer
- Thermometer
- Wine Thief
- Hydrometer
- Bag opener

PRIMARY FERMENTATION (DAY 1 TO 5):

2. Add 2 liters (half a gallon) of warm water to the Primary

- Sprinkle Bentonite into the water and stir vigorously with your spoon (or Fizzex) for about 30 seconds to break up the pieces and form a slurry

3. Carefully open the juice bag with your bag opener

- Add juice concentrate to the Primary
- Add 2 liters (half a gallon) of warm water to the juice bag to clean out any remaining concentrate
- Dump water from juice bag into the Primary

4. Add cool water up to the specified amount of wine (usually 23 liters or 6 Us gallons)

- Stir vigorously once again for 30 seconds to mix your wine must

5. Draw a sample of your wine must using your wine thief to verify that the specific gravity matches the amount from the wine kit (usually 1.080 to 1.100). Record it.

6. Put your floating thermometer into the must and record the temperature (should be 18-24 C/65-75 F). Record it.

7. Sprinkle oak chips (if included) onto the surface of the wine must and gently stir them so that they go just below the surface.

8. Sprinkle yeast package onto the surface of the wine must and do not stir.

9. Next, secure the lid on top of the Primary. Then secure the bung with the airlock (half-filled with clean water) in the hole on the lid.

Place your Primary in a room that is consistently between 18-24 C (65-75 F) and not in direct sunlight.

- Consider using that "brew belt" I mentioned above if you are making your wine in a colder room such as a basement
- If you have one loop it around your Primary in the middle section and then plug it in
- It will keep your wine must at a consistent 22 C (72 F) and is only needed for the first 3-4 days of fermentation

10. Fermentation should begin in approximately 24-48 hours

11. Let the wine must ferment for approximately 5 to 7 days.

SECONDARY FERMENTATION (DAY 7 - 18):

12. Draw a sample of the wine must with your wine thief and check the specific gravity.

- The majority of the fermentation should have occurred, and the specific gravity should be 1.010 or less.
- If it isn't, then replace the lid and let your wine sit for another day and retest.

Remember, the _temperature_ of the wine must (and the room it is in) will dictate how fast the fermentation occurs, so if the temperature is below 18 C (65 F), your fermentation will take longer.

13. When the specific gravity of the wine must is correct, transfer it to the Secondary fermenter (i.e., the carboy).

- Do this by placing the Primary on a table or countertop approximately 1 meter (3 ft.) above the Secondary
- Transfer the wine into your clean and sanitized Secondary using your auto-siphon
- Be sure to leave the lees (sediment) behind in the Primary
- Note that this will leave airspace in your carboy. Don't worry about it at this point as you'll need the space for the stabilizing and clearing step, which follows further on
- Re-attach the bung and airlock (replace the water) to the Secondary

14. Let sit for ten days till fermentation is completely done.

- *HINT:* If you are storing your carboy in a room where either natural light or light from light bulbs will be present, consider wrapping your carboy with a blanket, towel or old t-shirt cutting out the possibility of UV light, causing your wine to oxidize. It will also act as an insulator.

CLEARING & STABILIZING (DAY 18 - 26):

15. Draw a sample of the wine must with your wine thief and check the specific gravity.

- At this point, the fermentation should be completed, and your specific gravity should read 0.996
- To confirm that the fermentation is complete, let your wine sit for another day and recheck the specific gravity. If it is stable at 0.996, then you are good to go. If not, then let it sit for another day and recheck.
- *Note:* If you are a little impatient and don't bother checking the specific gravity on the second day and get right to it after only one day, you risk your wine not clearing correctly. It means you might have a beautifully flavored Chardonnay, BUT you might not be able to see through it in the glass ...

16. Do some warm-up exercises as this is the stage where you will need to "stir vigorously" with your long spoon (unless, of course, you

have invested in one of those "Fizzex" attachments for your cordless drill).

17. Clean a glass measuring cup and add 125 ml (½ cup) of cool water. Dissolve the contents of package #2 (metabisulfite) and package #3 (sorbate) into the water. Remember, these will act as a preservative and will prevent the wine from fermenting any further.

18. Add the mixture to your carboy and stir vigorously for two full minutes. It will both ensure that you mix the above into the must nicely as well as drive off any lingering carbon dioxide. It will also stir the sediment back into wine must (this is fine and helps with clearing your wine).

If your kit came with a smaller foil bag (i.e., the "F-Pack" or "Süsse-Reserve"), now is the time to get it as you will be adding it.

- The purpose of the "F-Pack" is to add flavoring after the fermentation process has occurred and will not add any additional alcohol to the wine (unless of course, you re-ferment the wine must)
- First, remove approximately 50 ml (2 cups) of wine from the carboy using your wine thief to make room for the F-Pack
- Be sure to keep this wine as you may need it to top up your wine must during the aging process
- Second, shake the foil bag then carefully remove the cap using the handy dandy cap remover that you used to open the larger juice bag, then carefully pour the contents into the carboy

- Stir vigorously for a few minutes to mix the juice with the wine must

19. Draw a sample of the wine must with your wine thief and check the specific gravity.

- Depending on your kit your specific gravity should be between 0.998 and 1.005
- This higher specific gravity should be expected as you are adding more sugar back into the wine must and therefore the density of the liquid will increase

20. Grab package # 4 (the clear packaging with the chitosan or isinglass clarifier) and give it a good shake. Using scissors, cut one corner of the pouch, and carefully pour the liquid into the carboy.

- Remember, the purpose of the clarifying (aka "finning") agent is to clarify the wine must.
- It does this by literally pushing the sediment in the wine down to the bottom
- If you check the carboy each day as the wine clarifies, you'll see a distinct line of sediment being pushed down to the bottom.

21. Stir vigorously for a couple more minutes to mix the finning agent into the wine must and to further drive off any remaining carbon dioxide.

- You ultimately want to make sure your wine is "flat" in a similar fashion to Ginger Ale flattening if you leave the bottle open for a few hours.

Using the reserved wine from step 18 or cool water (if you didn't have a foil pack) top the carboy up to within 5 cm (2 inches) of the bung. It will prevent your wine from oxidizing and spoiling.

- Refill the airlock with clean water or a metabisulfite solution

22. Let your wine clear for another eight days.

CLARIFICATION & RACKING (DAY 26 – 54):

23. Your wine should be quite clear after approximately eight days, and this step will help "polish" it even further

24. Using your auto-siphon transfer your wine from the current carboy into a second clean and sanitized carboy ensuring that you leave the sediment behind

- If you do not have a second carboy you can rack (transfer) your wine into the Primary, clean your carboy then transfer it from the Primary back into the carboy
- Remember to transfer your wine; you will need to place the carboy with the wine in it on a table above the carboy that you are transferring to as this process works using gravity as its ally.

25. If you are planning on aging your wine for more than six months, some kits suggest adding a metabisulfite solution to prevent your wine from spoiling (consult your wine kit's instructions).

The Winexpert kits, for example, suggest adding 1.5 grams (¼ teaspoon) of the potassium metabisulfite to 125 ml (½ cup) of cool water and then gently (not vigorously) stirring this into the wine must.

You could also add this solution to the bottom of the carboy before you do the transfer and then rack (transfer) your wine into the carboy and allow the two liquids to combine this way.

The extra sulfite shouldn't affect the flavor of the wine.

Top up the wine to within 5 cm (2 inches) of the bottom of the bung as we did in step 21.

- You can either use cool water or a similar wine

26. Reattach the bung and airlock (ensuring that you have also replaced the water in the airlock)

27. Allow your wine to clear for another 28 days.

- Draw a sample of the wine out of the carboy with your wine thief. Then examine the clarity of your wine in a wine glass.
- If you are satisfied with the clarity, then you can either bottle

your wine OR continue to bulk age it in the carboy for three months to a year, depending on the type of kit.

- Some people prefer to age in the carboy while others prefer to age the wine in the bottle. I prefer to age it in the carboy so that you can ensure a consistent batch. I bottle when I'm ready to drink the wine, but then again, it is certainly up to you!
- If the wine isn't completely clear, then let it stand for a further seven days.
- Don't bottle cloudy wine and expect that it will clear in the bottle – it, unfortunately, doesn't happen that way!

28. You may also consider filtering your wine at this point.

- It is another personal choice, and the pros and cons are discussed further in this book

BOTTLING (DAY 54+):

29. Most wine kits will produce enough wine to fill 30 – 750 ml (25.4 fl. oz) wine bottles, and you will, therefore, need to ensure that you have cleaned and sanitized enough wine bottles ahead of time.

30. You may also consider racking your wine from the carboy into another carboy if you do not want any remaining sediment to be inadvertently added to one of your bottles

Note: This shouldn't be an issue if you decided to filter your wine in step 32 as you would have already removed any remaining sedi-

ment from the wine.

31. To siphon your wine from the carboy into your wine bottles, you will need to place your carboy on top of a counter. You will also want to add the bottle filler to the tubing of your auto-siphon.

- I suggest you do this part with a second person so that you can have a little production line going
- One person can be in charge of filling the bottles while the other person hands them the bottles and takes care of the corking portion as well
- The person filling the bottle can sit on a little stool and either places the bottle on a little table or sit on the floor. Make yourself comfortable as you might be there for a bit.

32. To fill the wine bottles, insert the bottle filler into the bottle and press down to start the flow of wine. Pull up on the bottle filler just before the wine reaches the top.

- One nice feature of the bottle filler is that it displaces the perfect amount of wine so that you have a nice two-finger space from the top of the bottle once you remove it.
- This space is essential so that you can insert the cork into the bottle and still have some space for any gas remaining in the wine to go

33. Hand the bottle to your "corker" who will use either the hand corker or floor corker to insert the cork

- Ensure that the corks are clean and sanitized before you insert them. Consider rinsing them in clean water and soaking them in metabisulfite solution first.

For the Hand Corker: If you are using the hand corker, place the bottle on a stable surface, insert a cork into the top of the corker then place the bottom end on top of the wine bottle. Next, push the two levers all the way down until the cork is fully inserted into the bottle.

For the Floor Corker: Push the bottom of the bottle down on the spring-loaded platform and insert the neck of the bottle into the cork receiving area. Insert your cork into the hole above the neck of the bottle then push down on the lever to insert the cork. Certainly a lot easier than the hand corker!

NOTE: Some local wine kit stores rent floor corkers if you don't want to buy one.

34. For the first three days, store the bottles upright and then lay them down on their sides to keep the cork moist for aging and until you drink them.

- Store your wine in a cool, dark and temperature stable room

35. Enjoy!

There it is in a nutshell!

Your instructions should be relatively close to these 35 points with a few alterations here and there. If you are unsure, refer to these 35 points, and you should be FINE.

STEP THREE: LET'S GO BOTTLING!

THE WINEMAKING PROCESS IS FINISHED, SO TIME TO BOTTLE YOUR WINE!

LESSON 7: TO FILTER OR NOT TO FILTER – THAT'S THE QUESTION!

One of the more interesting conversations you'll have with fellow homemade winemakers is their take on filtering the wine before you bottle it as there are many opinions on the subject. I have done both, and from a sheer "easiness" factor, it is an extra step that I'd rather not do, mainly because of the extra effort that goes into doing it.

Pros:

- Your wine will look better / clearer
- Your wine will taste better
- Reduces the risk of spoilage
- Reduces off-flavors and aromas

Cons:

- It can be very costly
- It can be time-consuming
- You may have to buy filters often
- It can strip flavors, aromas, and colors

THE MAIN GOAL OF FILTERING THE WINE:

The main goal of filtering the wine is to remove any extra sediment such as dead yeast, vitamin B, bentonite, and other suspended solids that remain in the wine before you bottle it.

In other words, you are looking to clear out items that you wouldn't typically want in your wine glass. I believe that if you let the wine age for a reasonable amount of time (say six months to a year) and rack it several times during the aging process, you will remove the majority of those unwanted items anyways as aging gives the wine time to settle out.

You might find that filtering affects the flavor of the wine and strips some of the color out of it as well.

THE EFFORT NEEDED TO FILTER YOUR WINE:

Filtering can be as simple as running your wine through a coffee filter. It works rather well and does not usually affect the color or taste in any significant way. It is not very efficient, though, and it can allow smaller particles that a wine filter will not allow through. It can also be a very messy process (what part of winemaking isn't).

There are different types of filters available to the winemaker at home. There is a basic unit that uses gravity. The wine passes down a tube through the filter chamber, and the filtered wine passes to another bucket or carboy.

The other possibilities are hand pump and CO2 cartridge systems. These are more costly, but the process is quicker.

Finally, the most expensive way is to use a commercial-type electric filter such as the popular *Buon Vino*. It pumps the wine through a system that has a few filters stacked to promote the maximum filtering of the wine.

Again, these are not selective, and you can risk losing the color, flavor, and aroma of a wine. The price of such a system is more than most winemakers can afford ($150 and up). The filters are even more expensive than the gravity-fed kind. These filters, once used, are not reusable and, therefore, will have to be tossed into the garbage after they have been used.

Your ancestors never filtered their wine, and they quite enjoyed it. It is up to you how much trouble and money you want to invest. You can produce wine that is so clear you can read a newspaper through it, and you do reduce the risk for some types of spoilage. It is totally up to you and what you want your wine to look like. If you do not filter, you will have a small amount of sediment at the bottom of the wine bottle after the wine ages. Just make sure that you do not shake or turn the bottle too much before serving, so the sediment will remain at the bottom.

TO FILTER OR NOT TO FILTER - ONE MAN'S QUEST TO FIND OUT:

I had an interesting conversation one Saturday morning with a gentleman by the name of Myron, who worked at one of the local wine equipment stores I frequent. He has made wine for the last 11 years and has, therefore, had the opportunity to see both sides of the coin when it comes to wine filtering. Myron told me about a test he did on an Australian Shiraz he had finished making where he filtered 24 of the 30 bottles and left six bottles unfiltered as he was interested to see if there was a difference.

Is "stressing a wine" possible? Filtering is one of the harshest things you can do to wine as you are squeezing the wine molecules through a small membrane under pressure, and it, therefore, stresses the wine.

Any time a bottle of wine is moved, transported, or shaken, the wine gets "stressed."

Myron contends that when a wine is stressed, the flavors will go into hiding, so the aroma and taste of the wine seem to be somewhat dull or muted.

As an interesting exercise, why not see if you believe him by taking two identical bottles of wine and vigorously shake one then do a taste test between the two and see if there is a difference.

Back to Myron's experiment ...

After he bottled the wine, he tried the filtered wine side-by-side with the unfiltered wine, and here is what he noticed:

At the beginning:

- There was a huge difference.
- The unfiltered wine had lots of flavor and was a pleasure to drink whereas the filtered wine had no flavor at all most likely because it was stressed due to the filtering process

One week later:

- The non-filtered wine still had more flavor than the filtered wine

Three weeks later:

- The difference wasn't noticeable

One month later:

- The filtered wine was smoother than the unfiltered wine

Myron's Conclusion:

Don't Filter If ...

- You like a full-bodied wine (such as red wine)
- Let it clear on its own and rack it several times

Filter If ...

- If you like a "smooth" wine
- Let it sit for a month or so after filtering it to allow the wine to mellow out and "de-stress."
- Also, a good idea to filter fruit wine so that you can remove any pulp leftover
- White wines are also more delicate and present much better if they are crystal clear

In conclusion, if presentation, smoothness, and clarity are important to you, then filter your wine; otherwise, don't worry about it!

Note that once you have filtered the wine, it no longer needs to clear and just needs to age.

LESSON 8: JAZZING UP YOUR WINE BOTTLES

O nce your wine is ready, it can look pretty plain and not very impressive. Here are some tips to jazz up your wine and personalize it.

THE BOTTLE:

Bottles come in every size and color. You can pick unique colors to add some flair to your wine. Just make sure you get them back when your friends are done.

Don't let them turn them into hippy candle holders. RECYCLE!

CHEAPEST OPTION (FREE):

Keep empties from your store-bought wine, ask your friends and family for their empties or buy them at your local bottle depot.

I clean our store-bought wine bottles shortly after using them, so I don't have to clean them all at once.

Labels are relatively easy to come off if you soak them in warm water for an hour or two. Then use a razor blade attached to a handle to scrape the wet label and glue off (available at your local hardware store in the windows section as they are used to scrape tape and dirt off of windows). I then use a sponge with a scouring pad on it to remove any remaining evidence of the label. Be sure to clean and sanitize the inside of the bottle as well.

Another alternative is to go to your local bottle recycle depot and see how much they would charge for a dozen bottles of wine. The upside is that you can usually buy a dozen for around $2, and they'll come pre-sorted, so the chances are that they will all look the same. The main downside is that they most likely came from a catered event such as a wedding and were used as ashtrays, so be prepared to roll up your sleeves and do some cleaning!

TYPICAL OPTION ($1 PER BOTTLE):

Typically people would rather start fresh and opt to buy brand new wine bottles, which are available at all wine equipment stores, supermarkets, and Costco's of the world for around $1 per bottle.

Capsules (aka "shrinks") and Caps:

You can buy several different caps and capsules to go on top of your bottle. Capsules are little wrappers that tighten when hot air is applied (a hairdryer works well for this).

Hot water works nicely as well.

They come in all different colors and styles.

The caps are plastic and fit right on top of the bottle.

They also come in many different colors.

NOTE: Adding a shrink is for decoration only and will not have much of an effect on keeping your cork moist.

CORKS:

Corks can come in different designs and, your friends will be impressed when they pull them out. Some corks can be personalized at specialty wine supply stores.

Natural and agglomerated corks will run you in the $4 to $5 range for 30, whereas synthetic will be in the $10 range for 30.

The main determining factor in choosing a cork for your wine is to decide how quickly you will be drinking your wine. If you will be going through your wine relatively quickly (within a year or two), then going the cheapest route (i.e., agglomerated) is your best bet.

The type of wine you are bottling also plays a factor since white wines typically don't age well, so a cheaper cork will suffice. A red or wine made from fruit typically age much better, and therefore going with a natural or synthetic cork should be considered.

Typical Cork Life Span:

- Natural Cork - up to 5 years
- Agglomerated - 2-3 years (depending on the length)
- Synthetic - 3 to 5 years

The main drawback of natural corks (apart from the fact that it is becoming increasingly more difficult to find) is that they sometimes have cracks on the inside or outside of it and they might impact the seal.

Synthetic corks, on the other hand, are consistent, and you can store the wine bottle standing up as keeping it moist is not an issue.

You will need to use a floor corker (instead of a hand corker) for natural & synthetic corks as you have to compress them to a larger degree then a hand corker will allow.

It used to be that you had to soak corks in a sulfite solution for 30 minutes to sanitize them but not anymore as they are much cleaner and typically come in a vacuum-sealed bag.

LABELS:

You can buy pre-made labels. Some of these are blank and can be customized on your computer's printer. These labels are pre-gummed, which means that you apply some water and stick them on.

You can also make your labels with computer paper. Print them out as you would labels and then cut them out.

You can use Elmer's glue to put them on. It's not recommended that you use real address labels as these are hard to get off when you finish.

The sky's the limit to what you can do with labels. You can make special ones for the holidays or special events for your friends.

Remember, you CANNOT sell your wine unless you like to continue your winemaking endeavors in prison!

There are also several companies online who can do all the work for you if you are interested in getting custom wine labels done. A quick Google search for "custom wine labels" turned up the following websites:

- Stoney Creek Wine Press – www.StoneyCreekWinePress.com
- StickyBusiness – www.StickyBusiness.com
- 4th & Vine - www.4th-vine.com
- Vista Print – www.VistaPrint.com

STEP FOUR: STORING YOUR WINE

STRATEGIES ON ENJOYING YOUR WINE DOWN THE ROAD

Lesson 9: Aging Your Wine So That Each Bottle In The Batch Tastes Like The Other

Lesson 10: Wine Storage Basics to Advanced

LESSON 9: AGING YOUR WINE SO THAT EACH BOTTLE IN THE BATCH TASTES LIKE THE OTHER

Most wines certainly improve with age, but aging requirements will depend on the grape. White wines typically do not age well (i.e., past one year), but red wines do improve with age. Aging allows for the wine to develop its flavor. It also allows some of the chemicals involved in the winemaking process to dissipate.

There is a difference in opinion on whether to age your wine in the bottle or carboy (also known as "bulk aging"). Some don't believe bulk aging makes a difference, while others do.

Those who believe it makes a difference argue that:

- Wine doesn't clear in the bottle due to the lack of space in the bottle

- Vineyards age their wine in barrels so it must be a good idea to bulk age
- Aging in a carboy makes the whole batch consistent since it is done together
- Shape, color and amount of airspace in a bottle may influence aging as well
- Bottle when you are ready to drink the wine
- Aging in a carboy also prevents you from drinking the wine too soon
- You will need more carboys then wine bottles

When bulk aging your wine in a carboy, make sure your airlock doesn't get accidentally knocked off and that your sulfite levels are maintained to prevent outside bugs from ruining your wine.

Either way, you'll want to age your wine to get those complex flavors, and there are several ways you can do it. You can age them in barrels, a carboy, or bottles.

OAK BARRELS:

These usually are available in three types of oak - American, French, and Hungarian (based on where the wood was harvested). Oak barrels are VERY expensive. You also need to make large quantities of wine (30+ gallons) at one time. You can buy used ones from wineries, as over time, they lose their flavor and do not seal as well.

If you buy them new, they will ask what kind of char you want. It means that they burn the inside.

For home wine, it is recommended that you use a "medium char." You CAN ONLY use white wine in a white wine barrel and a red in a red wine barrel. It is because red wine can change the color of white wine if they are aged in the same barrel.

Here is the traditional method of oak barrel care when you intend to use them quickly (within 24 hours):

- Stand the Barrels upright
- Fill with 5 gallons (19 liters) of cold or warm water (80°F to 120°F – 27° C to 49° C) in each barrel.
- Turn the barrel on its side, roll it to wet the inside surface of the barrel thoroughly, and then stand it on the other head.
- After 4 to 5 hours, turn the barrel again, so that it is once more standing upright.
- The next day, check to see if the barrel is free of leaks. If some leakage is apparent, repeat steps 1 through 4. If there are no apparent leaks, proceed to fill the barrels with wine.

Storage of Barrels:

If the unused wine barrels are to be stored for an indefinite period, keep a plastic film on the barrels to prevent them from drying out.

When you are ready to use the barrels, follow the above steps. When barrels are not being used, they must be stored full of a mild sterilizing solution to prevent cracking & drying.

Every two months, replace the solution or add more sulfite.

If your barrel leaks and it is used, it may be time to discard as the barrel may be beyond its usefulness. Mind you; you can certainly cut it in half and use it as a flower planter (if you are both a handy type and a green thumb).

CARBOY:

To avoid spoilage in the carboy, ensure that the carboy is full and has the least amount of airspace at the neck as possible.

You'll also want to ensure that you keep your carboy in a cool, dark place where the temperature is relatively consistent, AND you'll want to keep an eye on the amount of sulfite in the carboy. It will ensure that if any bugs do get into your wine, the sulfite is there to control them.

To measure the amount of sulfite in your wine, go to your local wine-making supply store and buy a sulfite testing kit. They'll also be able to tell you how to use it properly.

BOTTLES:

We'll talk more about the storage of bottles in the next Lesson. For now, place them in a cool, dry, dark place.

*HINT: **If you store your bottle horizontally**, you may want to store a couple of the bottles vertically so that you can serve it to your guests.* If not, when you turn the bottle upright, you'll dislodge the sediment, and it will be floating in the bottle.

LESSON 10: WINE STORAGE BASICS

In order to keep your wine to its fullest potential, storage is essential. You must pick a place in your home that's:

- Clean
- Cool
- Dark
- Dry

A basement is a good place as long as it is dry. If not, your corks may turn moldy and therefore ruin your wine. Consider using a dehumidifier if your basement is damp, although you don't want it too dry because this can dry out the corks and cause them to shrink and crack. Light (more specifically, the UV rays) can damage your wine as it can cause it to oxidize more rapidly. Try different places in your house to see what space works best for you.

Also, keep in mind that wine doesn't store well if in an area where the temperature varies a lot. Therefore storing it in a room close to an outside wall is not recommended (unless it is properly insulated and has a constant temperature).

If you are using a natural or agglomerated cork, ensure that you store your wine on its side so that you keep the cork moist via contact with the wine. A dry cork means that it will shrink, allowing air into your wine. Air will spoil your wine.

It is also a good idea to store your bottle with the label facing upwards for several reasons:

- You can see your label
- You won't ruin your label
- Ensures that any remaining sediment will rest on the opposite side so you will be able to read your label

You can buy storage racks. These look nice and hold the wine in such a way that the corks remain moist. Only turn up the bottles when you are ready to drink them.

You can make storage units with kits or plans from a local hardware store. These can be as cheap or as expensive as you like.

Probably the cheapest way to store wine is in wine bottle boxes with the dividers placed on its side

Ikea also has some cheap utility shelving with wine rack shelving that can be purchased as well.

There are large container units that can be climate controlled as well and can hold from 10 bottles to hundreds depending on the size. You can also get units that are filled with nitrogen gas. This gas creates a barrier that microbes that cause spoilage cannot live in.

You can inquire at local storage unit companies. Some offer storage units for wine, which is a good option if you have a small place and want to make a lot of wine.

If you are interested in "doing it right" then consider having a look at the wine rack options at Rosehill Wine Cellars (www.RoseHillWineCellars.com) as they have several wine cabinets, wine racks, and wine cellar cooling units that may interest you.

STEP FIVE: SO YOU THINK YOU'RE A VINTNER – TRY THIS!

IF YOU'VE BEEN MAKING WINE FOR A WHILE, HERE ARE SOME IDEAS TO ADVANCE YOUR WINEMAKING SKILLS!

Lesson 11: Equipment Upgrades

Lesson 12: How to Make Homemade Wine From Fresh Grapes

Lesson 13: Blending Homemade Wine – The Keys to Creating A Truly Unique Wine

Lesson 14: How to Make Homemade Wine From Fresh Fruit

Lesson 15: Some Final Thoughts

LESSON 11: EQUIPMENT UPGRADES

I mentioned some of these items above, but here is a recap on some items you may want to upgrade, which will make your winemaking efforts a whole lot easier:

Fizzex:

It is an attachment for your cordless drill and makes "stirring vigorously" so much easier!

Available at most winemaking supply stores.

Short Garden Hose:

I purchased this at a hardware store and makes rinsing equipment (especially buckets and carboys) so much easier.

Wine Bag Decapper:

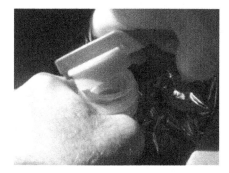

I received this as a promotional gift from one of the winemaking supply stores I frequent.

It's free marketing for the store and makes removing caps from the juice bag much more manageable.

You'll see what I mean after you've done it once using just your fingers or a screwdriver.

Plastic Funnel:

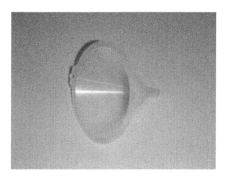

It is a typical funnel you'd purchase at a kitchen supply store and is useful when adding liquid to carboys.

EXTRA CARBOYS, AIRLOCKS, AND BUNGS:

They are especially useful when racking your wine and if you decide to have several batches of wine on the go at once.

Floor Corker:

It is about a $50 -100 purchase. After you use one, you will wonder why you did not buy it sooner. It makes corking easier, less messy, and much quicker.

Filtering System:

They can be pricey, but will produce a clearer wine.

* * *

Bottle Tree:

It is a unit to store drying bottles. You can also put sanitizer in the top bowl, and it will inject it into the bottles. It is a useful storage and cleaning device.

* * *

Stainless Steel Fermenter:

It provides ease in winemaking and allows for larger batches of wine. In some cases, this will eliminate the need to rack wine or put it into a carboy.

Bottle Cleaner:

It cleans bottles and carboys easily with high-pressure water. It is an effective way to rinse your bottles after you've cleaned them with sanitizer. They attach to most kitchen sink faucets and are available in either metal or plastic.

The Bottle Cleaner is spring-loaded

Put the neck of the bottle over the bottle cleaner ...

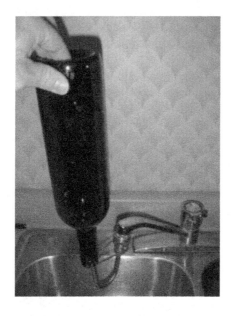

... and press down. The water will "blast" the inside of the bottle.

Grape Crusher and Grape Press:

They crush your grapes or fruit if you're making wine from scratch versus from a kit. A bladder press is optimum but not recommended for the home winemaker because of its cost.

LESSON 12: HOW TO MAKE HOMEMADE WINE FROM FRESH GRAPES

The process of making wine directly from grapes is a different process than creating it from concentrate. I don't recommend that a beginner winemaker tackle this as one of their first wines. Wine kits and extracts take all of the guesswork out of winemaking. The kits have been tested many times to work out the proper proportions of ingredients.

Creating wine directly from grapes is like creating a potion in a mad scientist's lab. Some things will work, and some will be awful. There is a lot of extra work involved and a lot of patience that is needed. Your first couple of attempts will be palatable if you're lucky. The more experience you've got working with kits, the better off you'll be in creating wines from scratch.

I don't want to talk you out of trying to create your wines; I just want you to go into it with the correct mindset. There is more time involved from start to finish. If you plan to grow the grapes, then you must understand that it'll take a few years before the grapes will be ready to make wine, unless you have vines that were planted years ago. Even then, it may take some work cultivating them.

You'll also discover that you'll have to buy (or rent) some more equipment. Depending on how big an operation you chose to have will determine the amount of money to spend. Be sure that you check with your local and federal laws concerning how much wine you can produce in a year, as this may be a determining factor.

To make wine from grapes, you have two options: buy grapes or grow grapes.

BUYING GRAPES

The grapes that you find in your local grocery store are great for eating. They come in a few different colors and varieties, and they're often seedless. They have thin skins and are sweet. These grapes are not the type of grapes that you would use to create wine. They're cultivated solely for eating. They look and taste a certain way because they were bred that way. Certain hybrids were created because people liked the taste, convenience, and shelf life. The problem is that some of the genetic attributes that are necessary for a good wine grape are bred out of the eating grapes.

If you were to bite into a wine grape, they would be sweet, but very chewy and have large seeds in them. The skin is also thick and rubber-like. They're not the type of grape that you would sit and eat by the handfuls. Wine grapes contain tannins, which are essential to color and mouthfeel, especially in red wines. Occasionally a higher-end supermarket will have Scuppernong or Muscat grapes. These are good to use as wine grapes but are hard to find. Even if you do find them, they may be costly.

If you don't want to grow grapes, but still wish to create wines directly from grapes, you do have some options. If you live in one of the wine viniculture areas of the world, then you're in luck. You can go to the local vineyards and try to broker a deal to get some grapes. Sometimes they'll let you pick grapes that have been left in the fields. You may also buy some of their grapes. You should be able to get a decent deal on them compared to buying them at a store.

Check with your local vineyards as they sometimes have picking opportunities at harvest time. They may allow you to bring home grapes in exchange for your manual labor. Besides grapes, you'll gain a lot of beneficial information by talking to the vineyard owner and have the experience of dealing with grapes first hand. The more questions you ask, the better your experience in home winemaking will be. Many vineyard owners start at home just like you.

You can find some vineyards that will ship grapes to you as soon as the harvest comes in. It can be expensive, and you have to use the grapes, sight unseen without much of a guarantee. You're better off buying grapes you can see and taste. It could mean that you take a road trip to a vineyard during the picking season, which could be a nice romantic getaway for you and someone close.

Another place to look for wine grapes is the local farmer's market. You may find many different varieties depending on what the climate is like in that area. You'll find good deals, because like I mentioned earlier, wine grapes don't make very good eating grapes most of the time. People often buy these types of grapes for canning and cooking.

Later in this chapter, I'll describe what you need to look for in a ripe grape ready for picking. These same rules apply for buying grapes from a vineyard or market. You want to pick them at the perfect time of the season, and so it might take a couple of trips before the grapes are ready for picking and crushing.

GROWING GRAPES AT HOME

Growing grapes can be fun, but they're also a lot of work. There are several factors you should consider before buying vines. The first thing to consider is climate and geography. Grapes will not just grow anywhere, and that's why there are certain designated viniculture areas around the world. These are areas that are best suited for growing grapes.

Even if the conditions are right for one variety of grapes, they may not be right for another kind. Don't buy vines based upon just what you like; you need to base your purchase on whether they'll grow where you plant them.

Finding the grapes that best grow in your area may take some research on your part. I would suggest you look online to see what wineries are around locally and either look at what they offer or call them. They're the experts on what can grow locally.

To determine if you have the right kind of soil, you can buy a soil testing kit at your local garden supply store. If you live in an area that has a cooperative extension office or similar government agency, they can also test your soil and may be able to give you suggestions for the best types of grapes to grow.

Grapes generally grow in soil that has gravel, flint, slate, or is stony. It's the type of soil that most other farmers would not give a second look at. You don't want rich black soil to plant vines in. The classifications of soil that you're looking for are clay, sand, or silt. The best type of soil is a combination of all three. It must be able to drain well. You want a slightly alkaline soil, which can be corrected with the addition of gypsum if the soil is too acidic.

The soil depth should be at least 30 inches/76 cm because grape vines have deep roots. You need to pick an area that drains well. If there is standing water, it'll kill your vines. You should look for an area that has a slight slope to it. The premium place is ¾ up the side of a hill. You want to avoid areas that are prone to moisture and frost.

Now you must calculate the size of the land you'll need for planting and the number of vines to produce the amount of wine you desire.

HOW TO CALCULATE THE SIZE OF LAND YOU'LL NEED TO GROW GRAPES

A mature grapevine can produce between 8-12 pounds of grapes.

It takes about 12 pounds of grapes to produce a gallon of wine.

The best spacing for vines is about 6 feet apart in rows that are 10 feet apart.

Below is a formula for determining how many vines you would need to produce a certain amount of

gallons of wine.

> G= Gallons of wine
> N= Number of vines in a row
> R= Number of rows
> P= Pounds of grapes per vine
> A= pounds of grapes to make a gallon of wine

In our example, we will assume that your particular variety can produce 10 pounds of grapes per vine and that you want 20 gallons of wine.

$$(G \times A) / P$$
$$(20 \times 11)/10 = 22$$

That means you'll need at least 22 vines of that variety to produce 20 gallons of wine.

In this example, you would need to consider the following formulas to determine the size of your vineyard.

$$[(N-1) \times 6] + 12 = \text{Length of a row}$$
$$[(R-1) \times 10] + 12 = \text{width of the rows}$$

This formula takes into account for 6 feet around the vineyard to bring mowers and other equipment in. Once you have the width and the length, you then multiply the two to get the square feet of your garden space needed.

In our example above, you had 22 vines. You can add an extra vine or two on a row as needed, so let's look at four rows of five vines each.

$$[(5\text{-}1) \times 6] + 12 = 36 \text{ feet}$$
$$[(4\text{-}1) \times 10] + 12 = 42 \text{ feet}$$
$$36 \times 42 = 1,512 \text{ sq feet}$$

Measure your space by width and length, and this will determine how many gallows you can produce a year. Some other considerations are not to plant them near forests as this can affect the vines. Trees change the climate of the vineyard and are a growing place for fungus spores. Avoid planting them where there is a lot of wind.

ESSENTIAL EQUIPMENT YOU'LL NEED TO BUILD YOUR VINEYARD

For the most part, you'll need a shovel, a posthole digger, fence pliers, spinning jenny, tamper, and saw. There are different types of trellising systems that you can choose from as you must train vines to a trellis. Part of the reason is that they need light to grow flowers and eventually grapes. Grapes do well in full sunlight as opposed to shady conditions. Trellises allow for pruning as well, which is necessary as you're growing your grapes. Fungal diseases grow more readily in damp shady conditions than they do in full sun.

The branches must be off the ground because if the fruit touches the soil, it'll rot. Finally, weed control is much easier when vines are off the ground and out of the way.

Depending on the type of trellis system, you'll also need posts, wire, springs, ratchet, pliers and wire cutters, earth anchors, cross arms, wire fasteners, and wire splicers.

When creating your trellis system, you'll need end posts as an anchor and line posts will hold it all off the ground. The two most common materials employed for line posts are landscape timbers or steel T posts. Use of high tensile, 12½ gauge steel wire is necessary. Don't use lighter weight wire such as that used for electric fencing.

You can dig the holes with a post hole digger, or you can have them driven into the ground with a driver. You must match the right kind of trellis system with the right type of cultivar you're using. Each system deals with the type of growth patterns the vines follow.

Most American and many French-American hybrid cultivars grow downward; therefore, they're best trained on a trellis that pulls them upward. European or V. vinifera cultivars, on the other hand, grow upward and is best managed with an upward vertical shoot positioning.

If you have questions about what type of system to use, ask the suppliers of your vines what they would recommend or look for a local vineyard owner to help you.

GROWING SEASONS

Growing and cultivating grapes is a year-round process. Each season has work that needs to be done. The techniques presented in this chapter are basic and are presented to give you a simple understanding of the process involved. There are different types of pruning that are done, but you must know what you're doing. If you cut the wrong part of the vine, you'll destroy any chance of grapes growing that year. It's best to seek the help of other vineyard owners, extension office personnel, or seek someone out from a local university or college.

* * *

Autumn:

It is the time of year that the process will start the first year. You'll loosen the soil and prepare your vineyard. It'll take two to three years before your vines are mature enough to produce fruit to make wine. You'll be pinching off the buds the first year to discourage fruit growth. All of the energy in the plant needs to be focused on growing a healthy vine that can bear the weight of grapes. I'll finish the process of the life of a grape with autumn repeated at the end.

Winter:

You'll be preparing the vines for spring and clearing out any old-growth or debris under your vines. You'll protect the ground with ground cover to protect the roots of the vine. The vines remain dormant during this period.

Spring:

Sap will begin to concentrate where canes (part of the vine that comes off of the main trunk) were pruned the previous year. This period is known as "weeping" as the sap becomes visible in the pruned areas. It is the beginning of the vine's growth during the coming season. This process begins when the ground temperature is at 50 degrees Fahrenheit (10 degrees Celsius).

Sometime in April or May, bud break occurs. It happens after the vine pools its energy for growth in the upcoming year. It is a particularly tricky time because late spring frosts can kill the newly formed buds and reduce or destroy that year's yield.

In late March and April, early grape development occurs. Sugars are not formed yet, but the maximum yield for that year is determined.

* * *

Summer:

In the late spring/early summer is when flowering occurs. During this period, the grapes are pollinated and are still very vulnerable to frost. After the period of flowering fruit, set occurs. It's during this period that grapes begin to mature. The grape flesh and skin tannins begin to develop. Fruit that's not maturing at a steady rate is pruned during this period.

During the late summer and early fall, the grapes will begin to change color. This period is known as "veraison." During this period, extra grape clusters are pruned as well as thinning the canopy so that sunlight can reach the fruit.

Autumn:

We return to autumn once again. This time your vines are mature and have borne fruit for harvest and typically occurs 100 days after flowering. This decision is based upon whether the fruit's genuinely ready to pick. If you pick them too soon or too late, they'll not be as good for winemaking. To determine when grapes are ready to be picked, you'll need to check the acid and sugar levels. One of the best ways to check if a grape is ready is to taste one. If they're sweet and not too sour, then they're ready to pick. You should wait an extra day, just to see if they get any sweeter.

To scientifically test a grape, you'll need an acid titration kit and a refractometer. You can then check both the acid and sugar of a grape to determine if they're at the levels you want for your wine. Both of these can be bought at your winemaking supplier. Check your recipe to see what level of sugar you would want for a particular wine. It determines the sweetness and the potential alcohol content of your wine. You need to have a balanced acid level in your wine, so you may need to adjust it by dilution or adding sugar or base to your wine.

You can use your refractometer when you check out grapes at your grocer or farmer's market. You can also use the taste test, but make sure that you'll not be breaking any laws by trying a grape!

When you pick the grapes, you should use sheers and cut them in bunches. Place them on sheets or in buckets. Try to get rid of any bugs or leaves as you're picking. I would suggest using gloves as some people's hands can get irritated by the tannins and acids in the grapes if you pick a lot of them.

You can also lightly rinse the grapes, to get rid of bugs and debris. Don't rub the grapes; just rinse them in a sink or outside with a hose. Rinsing them also removes sulfites, herbicides, and insecticides. If you want natural fermentation in your wine, don't rinse the grapes as you're washing away natural yeasts.

PROCESSING YOUR GRAPES

When you're creating wine from grapes, you must consider what equipment you already have on hand. Your primary fermenter should be at least 30% larger than the size of your finished wine. In the case of red wines, you'll need extra headroom because you'll be adding the skins at the beginning, and therefore it'll need room for the cap to rise. Your primary fermenter may not be large enough. You may consider, therefore, doing smaller batches or purchasing a larger fermenter. Remember, with wine from grapes, you must be prepared to create all of the wine all at once. You may want to call some of your winemaking friends over to join you if you have an overabundance of grapes. You can share the cost of some of the equipment, and you won't have grapes that go to waste.

One of the new pieces of equipment you'll need to consider buying for creating wine from grapes is a grape crusher/de-stemmer. This device is designed to crush the grapes and removes the stems from the pulp that's created. Stems don't make good wine.

There are various sizes and prices of crushers and de-stemmers, and many of them cost thousands of dollars. You may want to share the cost with other home winemakers. These devices can be manual, motorized, or you can purchase a crusher without a de-stemmer. You can look at places like eBay or Kijiji for some used models and get some good deals. Watch out for shipping costs as this equipment is heavy!

You do have the option of doing it the way your ancestors did, with your feet! The idea is to break the grapes open and release the juice. DON'T use a food processor or blender. It will destroy the wine and make it bitter. If you crush them using your feet, make sure you sanitize them or even enclose them in plastic before beginning.

The other piece of equipment that's essential for wine from grapes is a wine press. This device presses the rest of the juice from the grapes, without damaging the seeds, which will impart bitterness to your wine. These can vary in size and can be bought relatively inexpensively from winemaking suppliers and eBay. Buying a smaller press just means that you'll be doing more pressings.

In the next section, I'll go through the process of creating your wine from beginning to end. There are slight variations between red and white wine. The main difference is the leaving of skins in red wine.

Day One:

The first day you'll be processing the grapes, whether you bought them or picked them.

1. First, you'll rinse the grapes. Remove any rotten grapes or

clusters. Go over the grapes and make sure you remove any insects, leaves, or debris.

2. If you've got a crusher/de-stemmer, then you can skip this step. If you don't have a de-stemmer, then you'll need to remove all of the grapes from their stems by hand. You must do this before crushing them.

3. If you've got a crusher, then you'll run the destemmed grapes through it. Use a large spoon to mix them around. You'll find that not all grapes are the same and may vary from bunch to bunch and so you need to mix them well to get an even amount of sugar and acid throughout the must. If you don't have a crusher, you may do this by stomping them. Remember to clean and sanitize your feet often, and make sure you have a camera handy to catch the event.

4. Once you've mixed the must, you should perform an acid and sugar test. You can extract some of the liquid and use your hydrometer. You'll need an acid test kit to figure out the total acidity. Use your hydrometer for sugar and acid test kit for total acidity (TA). You'll need to decide whether you need to add acid and sugar or whether you'll need to dilute the mixture.

5. To raise the sugar content, you should add pure wine juice concentrate. Do this slowly and recheck your readings. Don't add table sugar, or it'll make your wine cidery. Most wine yeast is designed to die off at 12 to 14% alcohol. If your must is at 28% sugar, you'll end up with a sweeter wine than you might want. If you want to adjust the acid content, then you can add an acid blend. It will add a little life to the taste of

your wines. Your target acid should be .6 to .7% in red wines and .7 to .8% in whites.

6. Once you've made your adjustments, you'll want to kill off any wild yeasts that can ruin a wine. Add one-half teaspoon of metabisulfite for every 5-6 gallons of wine.

7. You want a slow fermentation while the skins are still on the must. You can create plastic zip lock bags with frozen water in them. Make sure you sanitize the outside of the bag. Allow the must to rest 24 hours so the sulfite can "gas off."

8. After 24 hours, add your yeast—one packet for every 5-6 gallons.

Day 2 to 12:

1. If you're making a red wine or maybe a blush, you'll want to do what is called maceration or fermenting on the skins. You'll need to "Punch down the Cap," which is pushing the skins that are floating back down into the juice a couple of times a day. You'll also need to replace your ice bags.

2. The longer you wait to press your wine, the more tannin and flavor will leech from the skins. When to press is a matter of taste. The color of your must will get darker for about seven days. After seven days, it'll become lighter, but there will continue to be tannins accumulating.

3. Don't press the juice from the cap on the day you're pressing your wine. Try to get as much juice from the wine without pressing at this time. The juice that you have is the premium juice. It'll make the best wine. The juice that you'll press in

step three will not be as good by itself. You can choose to separate the two or blend them. Unless you have a lot of juice at this step, it's recommended that you blend the juice.

4. It's at this step that you'll treat white and red wine the same. If you're creating a white wine, you would skip the maceration and go directly to pressing on the day you crush your grapes. Make sure that you sanitize your press before using it. When you're ready to press, add the pulp from your wine and use the press to squeeze the remaining juice.

5. Don't press too hard or you'll damage the seeds and add a bitter taste to your wine.

6. Once you finish pressing the juice, siphon it into your primary fermenter. You'll need to leave about 3% headspace for rapid fermentation. If you have not already added your yeast, do so at this time. You may also want to do a hydrometer reading. If you have some extra juice, seal them in jugs, without adding yeast to top off your wine during racking.

Day 40 to 60

1. Between 40 and sixty days from the time you started the wine, your fermentation will be completed. It includes both alcoholic and malolactic fermentation. You may choose to rack the wine at least once during this period. When you're sure it has stabilized, and you're happy with your hydrometer reading, you can move on to aging your wine. If you need to, you may top off the wine after racking with any juice that

you saved back. Make sure you add sulfite to the unfermented wine, or it can start up the process all over again.

Aging

1. Once you've racked your wine into your carboy one last time, you're ready for aging your wine. You want to remove your wine from the sediment from the bottom that's referred to as "gross lees." It is made up of mostly dead yeast and decomposing grape particles. This process is called autolysis, and if you let your wine stay on them too long, it can add weird, unwanted flavors to your wine.

2. In this last racking, you should add one-quarter teaspoon of potassium metabisulfite to every five gallons of wine. This addition to your wine will bring sulfite levels up to 100 parts per million (PPM). If you wish, you can also use a sulfite testing kit. It will ensure that your wine does not change color or have any unwanted yeast growing in it.

3. If you don't wish to barrel age your wine, you can add oak chips. If you're using an older barrel, the addition of some newer oak chips will enhance the flavor of your wine.

4. If you need to add more liquid due to evaporation, you can top off your wine with saved wine or a store-bought wine. You can add just a few cups of a similar wine without affecting the taste of the wine you're aging. Adding a few cups of store-bought wine will not change five plus gallons significantly, but try to buy a style close to what you're

making. Reducing air space is now very important! Don't use grape juice at this stage, especially if it has not been inoculated with sulfites.

5. You'll want to make sure that you age your wine in a cool environment, like a cellar. It needs to be in a place where the temperature is relatively stable. In France, they often use caves to age their wine. There is thermal protection in volume. If your wine room changes 10 degrees overnight, a 750 ml bottle will change 10 degrees, whereas a 50-gallon barrel might only change one degree.

6. Make sure you don't have airspace. You want to keep topping off your wine. Air means oxygen, and oxygen will destroy your wine. You must wait to bottle all of your wine at once. If you take out wine, you'll add that much more airspace.

7. After six months, you may want to rack it again, as some more material may have settled.

8. If you're having a problem clarifying your wine, you may want to look at the chapter on clarifying or filtering your wine. Remember that filtering can remove good things as well as bad. It can fade the color of your wine and flatten the taste.

9. If your wine tastes a little acidic, you can cold stabilize it. It means you need to make it even colder. You can put it in an old refrigerator. You want to get it as close to freezing as you can. The acid will crystallize, and you can then remove it by racking your wine.

10. If you find some carbonation in your wine, you need to

degass it. The simplest way to degass your wine is to stir the wine with a wooden dowel or a plastic rod. If you have the Fizzex attachment for your drill, use it instead (much easier on your arm). Stir the wine vigorously for about a minute and then replace the airlock and let the wine settle down for 30-45 minutes.

11. Once you're ready to bottle your wine, transfer it to your bottling bucket and make sure not to leave too much headspace in your bottles.

12. After bottling, be sure to allow the wine to settle a few weeks before opening.

TIPS ON AGING

Some people have questions about how long they should age their wine. Here are some suggestions based upon the type of wine you're aging. Keep in mind that if you're using barrels, you can use a barrel that you aged white wine in for either a white or red wine. If you age red wine in a barrel, you can only use it for red wines from then on.

- If you're aging full-bodied red wines, they should be aged for at least a year. If you can wait, two years is better and three years is ideal. Unless you have an iron will and great patience, you probably will not wait that long.

- If you have a light red or rosé wine, you should age them for at least six months. A year is even better.

- If you're aging a full-flavored white wine, try to age them for at least six months, but a year is better.

- If you decide to age a light, fruity white wine, you should age it for at least three months, but six months is even better.

SOME FINAL THOUGHTS ON MAKING WINE FROM GRAPES

I have presented you with the basics of making wine from grapes. You can start slow and buy grapes and press them yourself at home. Try this a few times and get the hang of using the fruit rather than just juice concentrate. After a few tries, you should be able to create delicious wines easily. You can even try your hand at blending wines. If you mix the grapes and press them together, you'll have less control over the final taste of your blended wine. You'll have better results if you create individual wines in smaller batches that you can then blend. The number of different combinations is infinite. You can refer to the chapter concerning blending for more instructions. You may want to try picking or growing your grapes. It can be fun, and you can involve your whole family. They'll enjoy picking and tasting the grapes. Be careful during your excursions as bees and other pollinators love grapes too.

SOME EXTRA RESOURCES:

- *For a full list of grape varieties,* please go to http://en. wikipedia.org/wiki/List_of_grape_varieties
- **To find vineyards where you can "Pick Your Own" grapes:** Go to *Google* and search for *"Wine Grapes PYO"* and see what comes up. Prices are usually quite

reasonable and sometimes include free crushing and destemming.

To find grape distributors:

- M & M Grape Co. - www.JuiceGrape.com
- Delta Packing – www.DeltaPacking.com
- Go to *Google* and search for *"Wine Grapes for Sale"* to see other grape providers.

BONUS RECIPE FOR A DRY RED WINE

Ingredients:

- 18 lbs. ripe red grapes
- 1 Campden tablet (or 0.33g of potassium metabisulfite powder)
- Acid blend, if necessary
- Table sugar, if necessary
- 1 packet red wine yeast
- Nylon mesh bag or cheesecloth

1. When the grapes are at about 22° to 24° Brix, the grapes are ready to harvest. If they are already harvested, then you may need to adjust the sugar content. In either case, the grapes need to be tart, sweet, and fresh.
2. Sanitize all equipment.
3. Remove the grapes from the stems and place them into a

fermentation vessel. You can put a nylon bag or cheesecloth and line the vessel as it will make it easier to remove the pulp later. You can use your hands or a potato masher and crush the grapes. If you have a fruit press, you can use this as well, but make sure you return the pulp to add the red color to the wine. Once you have mashed the grapes as much as you can, add your Campden tablet to the must. Place some additional cheesecloth over the top and allow the must to sit for an hour.

4. The temperature of the must should read about 70° and 75° F (21° to 24° C). If you need to raise the temperature, you can by wrapping the fermentation vessel with a blanket or using a brew belt. Once the must has reached the right temperature, it is time to test the juice.

5. Remove a sample of the must and test it with your titration kit. If you need to make adjustments add a teaspoon of the acid blend as you continue to test the juice. You are looking for a target of 6 to 7 grams per liter.

6. Next, you will check the sugar content. You will want to have a target of around 22° Brix (1.0982 SG). To raise the amount of sugar, add a tablespoon at a time. If the sugar is too high, then you can dilute it.

7. If you are using dry yeast, follow the instructions on the packet for adding it to the must. For most yeasts, you will boil water, allow it cool to about 80° to 90° F (26° to 32° C) and then add the yeast. Stir it gently and add it to the must.

8. Cover the fermentation vessel with the cheesecloth, set in a warm (65° to 75° F - 18° to 24° C)) area to ferment.

9. After 24-48 hours, fermentation should have begun. Make sure if the skins float that you "punch" them down with a sanitized spoon.

10. Once your must has reached about .998 SG, it is time to rack the wine. Squeeze the juice out of the nylon bag or cheesecloth and then discard the pulp.

11. After 24 hours, you can rack the wine off of the sediment into another vessel (carboy). If you need to cut down the headspace, you can add a similar, already finished wine to top it off.

12. Check your wine after ten days and then rack your wine into another carboy. You may top it off again if you like.

13. Allow the wine to settle and clarify for about six months. When it is clear, you should rack it into a bottling bucket. Fill the bottles and cork them.

14. You should store your wine in a cool, dark place and allow another six months before drinking.

LESSON 13: BLENDING HOMEMADE WINE – THE KEYS TO CREATING A TRULY UNIQUE WINE

One of the essential aspects of making wine is learning how to blend wine. Blending wine can be done in several different ways. There is a process that helps you decide the correct proportions to make the best wine possible, which I'll also share with you.

WHY BLEND YOUR WINE?

The blending of wine is a simple process as you simply mix one wine with another. The result is a combination of the flavors and characteristics of both wines. The real process is more subtle and involved, however. Commercial wineries use blending to create consistency in their wines. That way, every time you open a Merlot of a particular brand, it should taste close or the same as any other Merlot from the same winery.

There are many variables such as the taste of a particular vintage, the tannins in a particular barrel, or the sugar content of the grapes in a particular year that can change a wine's taste. Wines are mixed and compared to a wine used as a standard. It takes skill and a real understanding of why wine tastes as it does.

The motivation for someone making wine at home is a bit different. Home winemakers are less concerned about consistency and are more focused on taste. The home winemaker blends different wines to make the wine taste better. It is more of an art of refining.

WINE BLENDING MECHANICS

Believe it or not, there is an actual *science* to blending wines. Let's say that you want to change the acidity of a wine. If you combine two wines with differing acid levels, you can reach a particular goal. It takes an understanding of proportions. The same mechanical manipulation can help you to mathematically predict residual sugar, color, alcohol, and volatile acid. Unfortunately, math will not be able to predict how it'll taste. Being able to calculate the measurable features is an excellent place to start for a home winemaker to blend wines.

It's recommended that the home winemaker use the *Pearson Square* because it's a visual math tool that can help determine values when blending wines and it's a tool that <u>anyone</u> can use.

Pearson's Square:

	Acidity Level	Desired Level	Parts
Wine A	A (1.2)		D (0.4)
Desired Wine (Wine C)		C (0.8)	
Wine B	B (0.5)		E (0.3)

Let's look at an example of using this simple application:

Let's say that you have two wines, and one has an acid level of 1.2, and the other is 0.5. Let's also say that you want the end acid result to be .8. The top left corner (A) and the bottom left corner (B) represent the acid level of the two wines you are trying to blend. The center number in the square (C) is the desired acid level. The two numbers on the right are numbers that you calculate. Square D (0.4) is the difference between square A (1.2) and square C (0.8); also, the square E (0.3) is the difference between square B (0.5) and square C (0.8).

You now have the numbers 0.4 and 0.3, which creates a 4 to 3 ratio of the wines. When you blend these two wines, you will use four parts of the first wine for every three parts of the second wine to get an acid level of 0.8.

This simple calculation is already taking you down the road of creating the blended wine that you want!

SOMETIMES YOU HAVE TO BREAK THE RULES!

Remember that creating the wine you would like is a fine art rather than a hard science.

The following is a list of wine blending rules for the home winemaker. Like any art, some basic rules are allowed to be broken. They begin with the hard and fast rules and end with the more flexible ones.

1. *You should only try to blend wines that are decent to start with.* If you begin with wines that have many problems combining them may only make it worse and make a wine that is not palatable.

2. *Begin with the end in mind when blending wines.* Don't just start mixing wines with no idea what you are trying to change. Have a goal of altering the acidity, color, and residual sugar.

3. *When blending your wines, do it in small amounts.* Make sure you are using the same sized amounts that you are blending. When you are doing the blending, make sure you have a pen and paper to write down the proportions of the wines you are blending so you will know what formula to use. In the end if you have someone helping you can do blind taste tests.

4. *Blend only two wines at a time.* If you wish to add a third, make sure you are happy with the blending of the first two. Then add the third to the already blended duo.

5. *Always spit, don't swallow.* Do not do more than four trials a day. Your palate will begin to become tired, and you will not be able to taste, as well.

6. *Before you begin to blend large quantities of wine, wait a day.* Even if you think you've found the perfect combination, wait and taste it the next day. Winemaking and especially blending wine is an art that should not be rushed.

7. *Filter your wines after blending, not before.* Sometimes when two wines come together, they can create various precipitations. You never know when this can occur, so it is better to wait and filter after everything has been blended.

8. *Try to blend wines from the same year.* The results are better, and precipitation is less likely to occur.

9. *When creating a blended wine, try to use wines that are close in character.* You are trying to improve the taste that is a combination of two similar wines.

10. *If you're not sure what wines you should be blending and need some inspiration,* don't hesitate to head on down to your local wine store and have a look at what commercial wineries have come up with. They've already spent some time trying to figure it out so certainly worth having a look.

LESSON 14: HOW TO MAKE HOMEMADE WINE FROM FRESH FRUIT

This could be fruit from your backyard, from your friend or family's backyard or fruit from the farmer's market. When picking fruit, try to buy the freshest fruit available or grow them in your garden. Many winemakers have succeeded in making trellises and growing their grapes. It can be a family hobby as you plant, grow, and harvest the grapes or any other fruit.

If you're making a white wine skip to # 3

Once it's picked, try to crush and extract the juice right away (be prepared for fruit flies). You can use the spent fruit as fertilizer or compost.

You can find several exciting recipes in *Appendix G* of this winemaking manual.

One additional resource I do encourage you to buy is a book written in 1976 by Raymond Massaccesi called *"Winemaker's Recipe Handbook."* It is *purple* and will cost you under $10. I have also seen it advertised online for under $3, so you shouldn't have a problem finding it. It's filled with over 100 easy-to-use tested recipes, so it should keep you out of trouble!

I have made both the blueberry and crabapple wines and have tried the raspberry wine that a friend of mine made using the recipes in this book, and they were all excellent! Note that the recipes produce a gallon of wine so you'll want to calculate the number of ingredients you'll need if you want a larger batch.

Aside from pure economics, making wine from fruit other then grapes will open up a whole new world of wine to you.

Making wine out of fruit is essentially the same as making wine from grapes, so you are already ahead of the game.

You will also want to consider buying an acid test kit seeing that you are making your wine from scratch. The acidity level will influence your fermentation, so testing the wine must before you start is a good idea. You can purchase them at your local wine equipment store for under $5 and be sure to get the one that has a scale between 2.8 and 4.4. The ideal pH range for wine is 3.2 to 3.4, and if your wine must is outside of that, then you will need to add either an acid blend to increase the acidity level or calcium carbonate to reduce it. Consult your local wine store for their recommendations for the amount to add in your specific case.

LESSON 15: SOME FINAL THOUGHTS

Thanks again for purchasing **Master Winemaking!**! I'm certainly glad that you did, and I hope that you've found all of the information I have provided you both interesting, intriguing, and inspiring!

My ultimate goal is to help you increase your winemaking *savvy* so that you feel comfortable making wine as well as motivated to get started with your first of many batches!

I also wanted to invite you to visit (if you haven't already) my Blog (www.MasterWinemaking.com) as I update it regularly with new tips, ideas, videos, and opinions on winemaking.

Before we finish things off, I wanted to give you a couple of other ideas on things you might consider trying or thinking about once you have a few more batches of wine under your belt ...

TRY MAKING A HIGHER-END WINE KIT:

You will get a higher quality juice as well as more of it. The wine typically needs to be aged longer (6 months to a year), but you will end up with a bottle of wine that would rival a $50 bottle of store-bought wine, but at a fraction of the cost

Most wine kit manufacturers will produce kits of various levels of quality, and you can quickly tell what this is by two things – the size of the box and the price. The larger the box, the more juice you will have, and the higher the price, the higher the quality. The more expensive kits will produce a higher quality wine, but also typically require you to age it longer to flesh out the wine's complexity.

The other neat thing about the more expensive wine kits is that they may also contain different additives to increase the flavor and uniqueness of the wine. For example, I have seen some kits include freeze-dried grape skins and others with a "mash" of wet crushed grapes that you can add to the primary. Note that you typically would put these into a cheesecloth type "sock" so that you can keep the floating matter to a minimum. Some grape skins even come in a cheesecloth sock – pretty "fancy-schmancy" if you ask me ... :)

It would be worth pointing out that if you are the type of person who likes to enjoy a glass of wine with most dinners and go through wine quite quickly, making a more expensive wine might not be in your best interest simply because these wines are to be savored and enjoyed. They also take longer to age, so you should, therefore, consider going with a cheaper wine that is ready in 3 to 6 months rather than a year. You might also consider building up your cellar with a combination of cheaper wines (for daily consumption) and more expensive wines for those special occasions. It will ensure that you get the best out of both worlds.

MAKE WINE WITH YOUR FRIENDS OR FAMILY MEMBERS:

It could be to share in the enjoyment and cost or even "buddy-up" with a winemaking friend or two so that you each make a different wine kit then split the results once they are ready.

I like this idea for several reasons:

- For some, winemaking is a *social activity* where you can spend some quality time wine your friends or family member(s) and have a good time doing it
- *Financially* it makes sense, especially if you are trying a more expensive kit for the first time
- If you make a wine kit and your friend makes a wine kit, and then *split your batches* evenly between the two of you, it means that you'll have access to a wider variety of wine rather than 30 bottles of the same thing.

As the Chinese proverb saying goes, "many hands make light work." Ever notice how long it sometimes takes at various stages in the winemaking process? Ever wish you had someone helping you clean all those bottles? Having an extra person to help make wine certainly makes the wine process so much easier!

HOW TO STAY IN TOUCH

If you have any questions about winemaking, comments about either this book (if you loved it you would leave a review on Amazon – or wherever you purchased it from) or my Blog, please feel free to contact me:

Blog:

www.MasterWinemaking.com

Email:

Travis@MasterWinemaking.com

To Your Winemaking Success!

APPENDICES

SOME EXTRA WINEMAKING STUFF FOR YOU!

Appendix A: Common Wine Problems

Appendix B: Winemaking Recipe Card

Appendix C: Winemaking Resources

Appendix D: Evaluating Wine – A Tasting Primer

Appendix E: Wine Tasting Protocol

Appendix F: Guide on How to Present Your Wine Properly

Appendix G: Wine/Liquor Recipes & Tutorials

APPENDICES

APPENDIX A: COMMON WINE PROBLEMS

Stuck Fermentation: A must that will not even begin fermentation could have a problem with the yeast, problem with the must, or both. The yeast could be so old that it is dead. Buy new yeast. It can be temperature or not enough nutrients as well.

Sweet Wine: An overly sweet wine can be corrected in two ways; you can restart fermentation, or you can blend the sweet wine with a like dry wine. The resulting wine will contain more alcohol than before, but the excessive sweetness will be gone.

Colored Haze: The use of copper, zinc, iron, or aluminum items can cause white, dark, purplish, or brown hazes. If it is iron or copper, a few drops of citric acid will usually clear the haze. If zinc or aluminum, try fining with eggshells or filtering.

Darkening Wine: This is from oxidation. You need to add two crushed Campden tablets to each gallon of wine.

Failure to Clear: If you boiled the ingredients to extract flavor, color, or both and your wine fails to clear, you most likely have a pectin haze. Makes sure you use a pectic enzyme, or you can try a fining agent to clear. Most of the time, it will eventually settle out and clear on its own.

Lactic Acid Bacteria Haze: If you added malolactic bacteria for secondary fermentation and it develops a haze that is revealed as a silky sheen when the secondary is swirled, you have a lactic acid bacteria haze. When you are sure the malolactic fermentation is complete, treat with three crushed Campden tablets per gallon of wine.

Off-Colored White Wine: A slightly misty or off-color white wine can often be clarified and discolored using eggshells. Eggshells are first cleaned and then dried in an oven as this makes them brittle. They are then easily crushed into tiny pieces, and these are stirred into the wine. They will slowly sink and, over time, collect carbon dioxide bubbles absorbed in the wine. These will cause the eggshell particles to rise and eventually leave the captured bubbles at the surface, thereby allowing them to sink again.

Fingernail Polish Remover Smell: The wine is contaminated with ethyl acetate. There are three ways wine can become contaminated. (1) Ethyl alcohol and oxygen can interact to create acetaldehyde, which can react with oxygen to create acetic acid (vinegar). (2) Bacterial contamination of the wine (by acetobacter) can allow the creation of acetic acid. The key to prevention is maintaining an aseptic level of sulfur dioxide. (3) Finally, ethyl acetate contamination can be created by yeast under stress as well as by many bacteria besides acetobacter. In most cases, this wine is ruined and must be dumped.

Flat Taste: Absolute flatness is symptomatic of insufficient acid in the wine.

Mannite: A serious disease of wine characterized by a very bitter taste and caused by mannitic bacteria or mannite. Mannite can occur when there is too little acidity or when too much heat is generated during malolactic fermentation; therefore, fermentation ceases. Solution - dump it.

Medicinal Taste: The wine has a medicinal taste, caused by too little acid in the must during fermentation. Solution - dump it.

Metallic Flavor: Rarely, the use of canned (tinned) fruit or berries or even juices can result in a metallic taste to the wine made from such ingredients. Nothing can be done to correct this off-taste, but you can avoid the offending brand in the future.

Musty or Moldy Taste: This is caused by wine standing too long on the lees without racking. Add one crushed Campden tablet and 1/2 ounce of activated charcoal to each gallon of wine and stir with a sterile rod. Allow to settle 4-6 hours and stir again. Repeat the stirring procedure 4-6 times and then let sit undisturbed 24 hours. Rack through a double layer of sterilized muslin to catch minute charcoal particles.

Plastic Taste or Smell: This is caused by using a non-food-grade plastic container for the primary fermentation. Dump it and get food-grade plastic.

Rotten-Egg Smell: Hydrogen-sulfide gas manifests itself as the smell of rotten eggs. Try bocksin, if this does not help - dump it.

Sour Taste: The most common causes for a sour wine are (a) the fruit or juice spoiled before the wine reached a self-preserving 10% alcohol level, (b) a lactic acid bacterial infection soured the wine, or (c) a souring product such as lactose (milk sugar) or lactic acid was misused. Pick only fresh unbruised fruit.

APPENDIX B: WINE RECIPE CARD

Master Winemaking Recipe Card

Brand of Wine Kit: _____   Type of Wine: _____   Start Date: MM / DD / 20__

STEP 1 – PRIMARY FERMENTATION:

Date: MM / DD / 20__   Specific Gravity: 1.____   Temperature: _____ F / C (circle one)

Added Ingredients:

Type of Water: _____   Oak: _____   Other: _____

Comments: _____

STEP 2 – SECONDARY FERMENTATION:

Date: MM / DD / 20__   Specific Gravity: 1.____   Temperature: _____ F / C (circle one)

Comments: _____

STEP 3 - CLEARING & STABILIZING:

Date: MM / DD / 20__   Specific Gravity: 0.____   Temperature: _____ F / C (circle one)

Date: MM / DD / 20__   Specific Gravity: 0.____   Temperature: _____ F / C (circle one)

Comments: _____

STEP 4 – CLARIFICATION & RACKING:

Date: MM / DD / 20__   Specific Gravity: 0.____   Temperature: _____ F / C (circle one)

Your Aging Plan: In Bottle   In Carboy (circle)   Date Ready to Bottle: MM / DD / 20__

Comments: _____

STEP 5 – BOTTLING:

Date: MM / DD / 20__   No. of Bottles: ____   Filtered?: Yes   No (circle one)

HOW DID YOUR WINE TURN OUT?   Total Score: ___ / 20

Appearance: __ / 2	Sweetness: __ / 1	Comments:
Colour: __ / 2	Body: __ / 1	
Aroma/Bouquet: __ / 4	Flavour: __ / 1	
Volatile Acidity: __ / 2	Astringency: __ / 2	
Total Acidity: __ / 2	Overall: __ / 3	

>> Download and print additional copies of this form by going to:

www.MasterWinemaking.com/RecipeCard

APPENDIX C: WINEMAKING RESOURCES

F reebies:

- Blog - www.MasterWinemaking.com
- WineMaker Magazine - www.WinemakerMag.com

"How-To" Articles From JuiceGrape.com:

- Fall Yeast Parings - Red Varietals
- How To Make Red Wine from Fresh Juice
- How To Make White Wine from Fresh Juice
- The 7 Most Common Winemaking Mistakes
- Common Wine Faults and Flaws
- Easy Yeast Starter Procedure
- Guide To Selecting Winemaking Additives
- Guide to Selecting Yeast for Winemaking

- Useful Conversions Courtesy of Yeast Whisperer
- Proper Application of Barrel Sealing Wax
- Toasted Oak Liquid Tannins Info and Instructions
- Red Wines General Instructions
- Accuvin Malolactic Tests How-To Guide
- Caring For Your Barrel
- Citric Acid Barrel Preparation
- How-To Measure Titratable Acid

Wine Recipes:

- Recipezaar - Search for "wine" – www.Food.com
- EC Kraus - www.eckraus.com/wine-making-recipes.html

Wine Kit Manufacturers:

- Winexperts - www.winexpert.com
- RJ Spagnols - www.rjscraftwinemaking.com
- VineCo - http://vinecowine.com
- Mosti Mondiale - www.mostimondiale.com

Yeast Manufacturers:

- WineMaker Magazine's Yeast Strain Chart - www.winemakermag.com/referenceguide/yeaststrainschart/
- "Lallemand (Lalvin)" - www.lallemandwine.com
- "White Labs" - www.whitelabs.com
- "Wyeast" (pure liquid yeast) - https://wyeastlab.com

Online Winemaking Supply Stores:

- Clickabrew (Canada) - www.clickabrew.com
- EC Kraus (USA) – www.eckraus.com
- HomeBrewIt (USA) - www.homebrewit.com
- MidWest Supplies (USA) - www.midwestsupplies.com
- South Hills Brewing Supply (USA) - www.southhillsbrewing.com
- Home Brew Hop Shop (UK) - www.home-brew-hopshop.co.uk
- Art of Brewing (UK) - www.art-of-brewing.co.uk

Wine & Beer Making Gadgets:

- Wine Pod
- Tap-A-Draft
- Fizzex
- V-Shaped Primary

Wine Storage:

- Rosehill Wine Cellars - www.rosehillwinecellars.com

Oak Wine Barrel Manufacturers:

- Barrel Mill - www.thebarrelmill.com
- Barrels Unlimited - www.barrelsunlimited.com

Wine Filters & Bottle Fillers:

- Buon Vino Manufacturing - www.buonvino.com

Cork Manufactures:

- Nova Cork - www.abccork.com

Fruit Trees, Plants & Wine Grapes:

- Willis Orchard Co. - www.willisorchards.com
- M & M Wine Grape Co. - www.juicegrape.com
- Walker's Wine Juice - https://walkerswinejuice.com
- Delta Packing - www.deltapacking.com
- The Nursery At TyTy - www.tytyga.com

Wine Bottle Labels:

- Evermine for Everyone - evermine.com
- Stoney Creek Wine Press - www.stoneycreekwinepress.com
- StickyBusiness.com - www.stickybusiness.com
- 4th & Vine - www.4th-vine.com

APPENDIX D: EVALUATING WINE – A TASTING PRIMER

B y *Mary Baker* (Dover Canyon Winery)

Wine is meant to be enjoyed, but for many, approaching a glass of wine is still an intimidating experience. By using the following ten simple steps, you will be able to determine your flavor preferences, learn how to judge the overall quality of a wine, and feel confident about voicing your opinion.

During this course, I'll be asking you to taste and evaluate certain types of wines. The availability of wines in various markets makes it difficult, if not impossible, to choose specific wines that would be available to everyone. Still, we've tried to assemble a list with some widely available, affordable suggestions. You might have a preference for whites or reds, Australian or American, and you should begin with wines that are familiar to you. I hope, however, you will explore other varieties and regions during your exploration of wine. I encourage you to submit your own choices for future exercises.

Figuring out what you like is the point of this class. But when you exercise your newfound confidence and knowledge with your friends, remember that everyone will have different flavor preferences—some like white wines, some lean toward reds. Some people prefer bright, fruity wines, while others prefer tannic, or slightly spicy wines. Variety is part of the mystique of wine.

WINE RECOMMENDATIONS

To get the most out of this course, may we recommend the following wines:

- chardonnay
- sauvignon blanc
- pinot gris or pinot grigio
- riesling
- pinot noir
- merlot
- cabernet sauvignon
- zinfandel
- syrah

Here are some recommendations for "varietally accurate" wines from affordable producers. If you can't find these particular wines, ask your local wine shop for recommendations. Make it clear that you are looking for "varietally accurate" wines, in other words, an excellent example of a single grape varietal. For this course, we will not be tackling blends yet, but learning to recognize the distinct aromas and flavors that a particular grape contributes to a wine.

You do not need a bottle of each varietal to participate. Shop within your budget, and invite your friends to participate.

Chardonnay

- Argyle (Oregon)
- Catena (Argentina)
- Meridian (California)
- Wild Horse (California)

Sauvignon blanc

- Glazebrook (New Zealand)
- Geyser Peak (California)
- Mulderbosch (South Africa)

Pinot gris or pinot grigio

- Alois Lageder (Italy)
- Chehalem (Oregon)
- Erath Vineyard (Oregon)
- Hugel (Alsace)
- Livio Felluga Esperto pinot grigio (Italy)
- St. Michelle (Washington)
- Trimbach (Alsace)

Riesling

- Bonny Doon Pacific Rim (California)
- Chehalem (Oregon)
- Erath Vineyard (Oregon)
- Hugel (Alsace)
- Trimbach (Alsace)

Pinot noir

- Saintsbury Garnet (California)
- Leaping Lizard California)
- Louis Jadot (France)
- Wild Horse (California)

Merlot

- Blackstone (California)
- Columbia Crest (Washington)
- Valdivieso (Chile)
- Wild Horse (California)

Cabernet sauvignon

- Rodney Strong (California)
- Sebastiani (California)
- Valdivieso (Chile)
- Wild Horse (California)

Zinfandel

- Dry Creek(California)
- Ravenswood (California)
- Wild Horse (California)

Syrah

- Columbia Crest (Washington)
- Hardy's Stamp (Australia)
- Jacob's Creek (Australia)
- Lindemann's (Australia)
- Wolf Blass (Australia)

GLASSWARE

It will be helpful, but not necessary, to use new wine glasses for every wine you taste. The brand and style of the glass are not important, but for evaluating the color and aroma of the wines, standard stemmed wine glasses are preferable.

WINE-TASTING PROTOCOL:

Wine tasting is often more educational, not to mention fun when enjoyed as a group. Ask each guest to bring a bottle of wine and six wine glasses. Provide fresh bread cubes or baguettes and filtered water for your guests. If you plan on serving appetizers or cheese, ask your guests to evaluate the wines first and then try them again later with food.

For assignments 1 and 2, use the following procedure.

Trace six circles on the placemats and place a glass on each circle. Pour a 3- to 4-ounce sample of each wine. Mark the circles with the name of the wine. Study each wine carefully, using the following criteria. Then go back and re-taste the wines again to see if your perceptions have changed. Compare notes, and have fun!

1. Color of the wine

First, examine the color of the wine. Hold the glass against a white background and tilt it sideways—a white wine should be pale straw to deep gold, and a red wine can be anywhere from brick red to deep, plummy purple. Older wines may have a brownish tinge around the edge, which is perfectly normal in an aging wine, but it may also indicate that the wine has peaked in flavor. A tinge of brown will prepare you for the flavors of an aging wine, which can range from dusky cinnamon to a rich caramel effect. In a white wine, any tinge of brown is a clear warning that the wine may be too old; the lighter, more tropical flavors of white wine don't typically hold up well to the caramelized flavors that develop with age.

2. Swirling

Next, swirl the wine gently. This has two purposes. The first is to prove to everyone in the room that you are a wine geek (try not to splash wine on the person next to you). The second purpose is to aerate the wine gently. When you smell the wine after swirling, your nasal receptors will pick up more bouncing esters and molecules than if you sniff a resting wine. It is not necessary to give the wine the washing-machine treatment. Swirling your wine for ten minutes will only exhaust the wine and make the wine room attendants dizzy.

3. Nice legs

After swirling, lift your glass above eye level and watch the wine drip down the glass. (There is no real purpose to this exercise other than demonstrating that you know how to do it.) You'll see a thin film of wine cling to the glass, then gently release in long drips, called "legs." Wines with higher alcohol content have stronger surface tension and will cling to the glass more, having thicker "legs." Swirled water, for instance, has no legs, compared to swirled brandy, which has drips like cake frosting.

The alcohol content is relative to taste. At thirteen percent alcohol, a delicate white wine like sauvignon blanc may not have the necessary flavor to survive the hot mouthfeel of strong alcohol content. Still, a heavier chardonnay or red wine may balance the alcohol perfectly.

4. Aroma

Now it's time to smell the wine. Take your time and use your imagination. If it were not wine, but perfume in your glass, how would you describe it?

A well-crafted wine should give hints of the fruit flavors to come, ranging from melons, peaches, and pineapple in white wines, to plum, cherry, and cassis in red wine. Oak is often more evident in a wine's aroma than in its taste, and depending on the type of barrels used, you may also find esters of cedar, vanilla, or cinnamon from oak aging.

Although aromas of mint and herb are often attractive, wines should never have unusually "green" aromas like asparagus, fermented grass, or pureed baby food.

5. Fruits and vegetables

Next, taste the wine. Savor the wine and roll it around in your mouth before swallowing. Most people have habitual methods of chewing and swallowing that probably do not include all the tasting receptors. Make sure the wine hits the middle, sides, and back of your tongue, as well as the top.

What is your initial impression? Is the wine tart? Soft? Caramelized? Spicy? Take another sip, and close your eyes. If it were not wine, but food in your mouth, what would you be tasting? Just as a Bing cherry is very different from the vanilla-like Queen Anne cherry, every wine varietal is different and distinctive. White wines are often described as tasting like pear, apple, or pineapple. Red wines are compared to cherries, plums, and berries. Cold growing seasons and some vineyards impart slightly vegetal characteristics that may remind you of herbs or asparagus.

(Taster's Tip: If you like, you can also aerate wine by swizzling it behind your teeth for a moment. It is most appropriate for young, tannic reds as it aids in evaluating the fruit and longevity of the wine. It is, however, considered gross to do this in a restaurant, and it is very pretentious to do it with every wine, particularly whites.)

6. Toast and butter

After the fruit and vegetable comparison, look for toast and butter characteristics. Various yeasts and winemaking techniques can, if the winemaker so chooses, give the wine a lingering bread-like smell, or the sweet-sour lactic aroma of buttermilk.

Toasty, yeasty wines are often the result of allowing spent yeasts to remain in the barrel with the wine for a while, called "aging sur lies." Buttery and creamy aromas are the result of a process called malolactic fermentation, a secondary, post-alcohol conversion in which a specialized yeast changes the tart, green-apple malic acids of the grape into creamier lactic acids.

These characteristics apply mainly to white wines, as all reds are put through ML as a matter of course, and the deeper flavor and astringent tannins in red wines make sur lies aging more challenging to detect.

(*Taster's Tip: Sometimes barrels do not finish the malolactic conversion, or winemakers will put part of their barrels through malolactic fermentation, and then blend those barrels with non-malo lots, resulting in a wine with partial malolactic. You can ask about the percentage of ML in a wine, and with practice, you will be able to guess accurately.*)

7. Tannin

White wines have little or no tannin, which is a woody component extracted naturally from the skins and seeds of the red grapes. If you remember Boris Karloff craving his Tanna leaves in The Mummy, then you may have figured out that tannins are a natural preservative which facilitates the aging of red wines. (You should drink most white wines within four years of their vintage date—they lack the preservative tannins and will darken and caramelize with age.)

Although white wines are often completely dry, red wines taste even drier because the fresh tannins in a young red wine are very astringent. As these wines age, their tannins decompose in the bottle, creating an earthy effect and, one hopes, a more complex wine. The subject of aging reds before consumption is a controversy that has lasted for ages, but there is a straightforward guideline. If you like young wines, drink them young; if you like older wines, age them.

8. Oak

Now study the wine for oak. Can you smell it? Can you taste it?

Not all wines should be oaky—the delicate fruit flavors of light white wines can be overwhelmed by too much oak, and even red wine can sometimes smell more like furniture than fruit. The effect should be subtle—wines should not taste of pine, cedar, toothpicks, or planks.

9. Good Body

What is your overall impression of the wine's textural feel? Does the wine have body and structure? Were its components multiplexed and interesting? Did the wine titillate all the surfaces of your mouth, and seduce your sinuses? Or did it seem to stick to just one portion of your tongue?

Body generally refers to a wine's ability to satisfy a multitude of senses in your mouth. Structure implies that the wine has layers of experience—flavors that echo the initial aromas and lead into a lingering finish. Some tasters prefer a thick, viscous, high-alcohol wine, while others enjoy a wine that seems to expand on the palate, throwing out a joyous array of flavors, aromas, and teasing textures.

10. The Finish Line

Does the wine have a nice finish, a lingering sensation of flavor? Wines designed to be pleasant, fruity gulpers should leave a clean, brisk finish; more expensive wines designed for longevity should leave hints of intriguing, mysterious, and pleasantly spicy flavors, much like an expensive and well-designed perfume.

WINE EVALUATION FORM

What we wanted to do is give students who follow the course and use the form an easy way to categorize the wines they like and don't like and make it more likely that they buy wines they'll enjoy.

Here is the way the form works:

- For most of the elements in wines (fruit, oak, tannins, etc.), there is a scale from 5 to 1.
- For any given quality, "5" means that the element is strong or very evident; 1 means the element is barely apparent or not apparent at all.
- Thus, for body, a "5" rating would indicate lots of body; "1" would indicate a very light body. Likewise, a "5" under fruit would mean a big fruit presence, and "1" would be used for a wine where the fruit is not as apparent.

- Remember, you're not rating the wine according to how well you like the various elements, or how well balanced they are, just on how evident they are.
- You may want to fill out two (or more) forms for some wines – one as you first taste the wine, and one later on after the wine has "breathed" for a bit, or perhaps one on tasting the wine alone, and one with food.
- There's a bit of space in each section, and plenty in the margin, for taking notes. Don't hesitate to use it.

In addition to the scales for the various elements of the wines, there is a section to rate how well you liked the wine overall.

After you've tasted and "scored" a selection of wines on both scales, take a look at your forms and see if there are any common likes and dislikes you have. Do you enjoy lighter or heavier bodied wines? Lots of oak or none? Fruity or less fruity wines? Think about your preferences and use the knowledge the next time you visit your wine store – you should be better equipped to ask for wines with the qualities you enjoy, and you're probably more likely to end up with satisfactory wines.

Download a PDF version here:

www.MasterWinemaking.com/WineScoringSheet

* * *

WINE SCORING SHEET

Producer, type, and vintage:

Aromas	5	4	3	2	1
Fruit and herb flavors	5	4	3	2	1
Toast and yeast characteristics	5	4	3	2	1
Malolactic characteristics	5	4	3	2	1
Tannins	5	4	3	2	1
Overall impression of oak	5	4	3	2	1
Body	5	4	3	2	1
Finish	5	4	3	2	1
Food friendliness	5	4	3	2	1

Other notes:

Overall (choose one):

1   Pretty awful by any standards
2   Decent wine, but not my thing.
3   Enjoyable, I'll happily drink it, but probably not buy it
4   Really good wine! I'll keep an eye out for it
5   Great stuff! I'll make my kids mow lawns to pay for more!

MORE ON THE UC DAVIS 20-POINT SCORING SYSTEM:

The *University of California at Davis 20 Point Scale System Organoleptic Evaluation Scoring Guide For Wine* was developed by Dr. Maynard A. Amerine, Professor of Enology at the University of California at Davis, and his staff in 1959 as a method of rating the large number of experimental wines that were being produced at the university.

The Davis system is quite straightforward. It assigns a certain number of points to each of ten categories, which are then totaled to obtain the overall rating score for a given wine.

17 - 20 Wines of outstanding characteristics having no defects

13 – 16Standard wines with neither outstanding character nor defect

9 - 12 Wines of commercial acceptability with noticeable defects

5 - 8 Wines below commercial acceptability

1 - 5 Completely spoiled wines

Appearance (2 points) - The wine is given 2 points if it is brilliant, with no dullness, murkiness, or particles of sediment. If it is clear, but not flashing with light reflections, it rates 1 point. If full or cloudy, it gets 0.

Color (2 points) - Acceptable colors for white wines are varying shades of yellow, gold, straw. Flaws are any amber tones, indicating oxidation. A rosé can be a true pink, or because of its grape source,

184 | MASTER WINEMAKING

tinged with deeper red or orange. Overly violet tints, brown tints of amber, or deep red are faults. The color of red wines depends significantly upon the grape variety. Pinot Noir may be light enough to verge on transparency. Cabernet or Zinfandel will be deep red. Newer or younger wines will often have blue-purple edges, as older wines will show bronze edges.

Aroma and Bouquet (4 points) - Aroma is the sensory impression arising from the mouth with the assistance of the sinus chimneys. The bouquet is fragrance detected by the nose. Either may be vinous, smelling like wine, but without any grape variety characteristics. The intensity may be light, medium, or high. Negative factors are odors that can be described as alcoholic, excessively woody, moldy, or corked.

Volatile Acidity (2 points) - This is the term for Vinegary. Does the wine smell of vinegar? If not, it rates 2 points. A slight vinegar smell will rate 1 point. If it smells of vinegar, it rates 0.

Total Acidity (2 points) - Felt in the mouth, around the edges of the tongue, it is wine's refreshing zing. If low, the wine is flat, flabby, or soapy. It can be too high with unpleasant sharpness.

Sweetness/sugar (1 point) - Sugar and total acidity go together. Overly sweet for the wine's type is a fault, as is overly dry.

Body (1 point) - This is the wine's viscous nature identified as mouth-feel, also the binges, or alcoholic strength.

Flavor (1 point) - The flavor should correspond with the bouquet and aroma, being clean, fruity, full, or balanced. It should not be metallic, steamy, or alien in character.

Astringency (2 points) - Tannins give a wine astringency (or bitterness), and so does the wood in which wine is aged. Younger wines will be rougher than older wines. The ideal is mellow softness, velvet, roundness. A young wine is not discounted for natural tannin.

General Quality (3 points) - The only category for subjective appraisal, adjusting the score based on the wine's total performance.

ASSIGNMENT #1 - VARIETAL COMPARISON: WHITE WINE

Equipment for one:

- A glass of wine!

Equipment for six:

- 36 wine glasses and 6 bottles of white wine, all different varietals
- white paper placemats
- notepads and pencils or pens (or use the wine scoring sheet provided)
- bread
- filtered water

In the wine business, they refer to each variety of grape as a varietal. Just as a vanilla-colored Queen Anne cherry differs from a blood-red Bing, wine grapes vary in color and flavor. Each type of grape has a distinctive flavor, and depending on where and how it's grown, specific characteristics of the grape will become more pronounced.

A winemaker's choice of yeast and winemaking techniques will also affect flavor, adding aspects of spice, pastry, or butter, and the amount of time a wine spends in oak will impart additional aroma and flavor to the fruit.

There are thousands of wine grape varieties throughout the world, but here are a few of the more common white wine varietals.

Taste six white varietals and try to identify each varietal's core flavors.

GUIDE TO WHITE WINE VARIETALS:

Malvasia Bianca

A light, crisp wine with floral aromas and a core flavor of grapefruit. Good chilled and served with salads or spicy seafood.

Sauvignon Blanc

A light wine with grassy aromas like fresh-mown hay or clover, and flavors of tart apple, kiwi, or citrus. Very good with summer time appetizers, green salads, pasta salads, and minimalist seafood.

Pinot Blanc

Similar to a chardonnay, pinot blanc has a deep blond color and creamy mouthfeel with a definite pear flavor.

Chardonnay

A pleasant workhorse of a wine, chardonnay has fruity aromas and a core flavor of apples. It's made in a range of styles from minimal oak and bright fruit, to heavy oak or butter styles. It goes with a wide range of food, from hors d'oeuvres and salads to light meats and spicy pasta dishes.

Viognier

A tropical powerhouse, viognier is intensely fruity, and sometimes has a grassy finish. It generally has a high alcohol content, which in turn gives the wine a heavier mouthfeel that also appeals to red wine drinkers. The combination of high alcohol and fruit salad flavors sometimes makes the wine seem slightly sweet, even when it is technically dry. Served chilled, it can stand up to very spicy dishes.

Other white wines to try include pinot gris, Roussanne, Marsanne, and Semillon.

ASSIGNMENT #2 - VARIETAL COMPARISON: RED WINE

Equipment for one:

- A glass of wine!

Equipment for six:

- 36 wine glasses and 6 bottles of white wine, all different varietals
- white paper placemats
- notepads and pencils or pens (or use the wine scoring sheet provided)
- bread
- filtered water

Taste six red varietals and try to identify each varietal's core flavors.

GUIDE TO RED WINE VARIETALS:

Pinot Noir

Although lighter in tannins than other red wines, pinot noir is packed with flavor. Its core flavor of cherry pie is accompanied by flavors and aromas of mushroom, hay, cinnamon, pastry, and oak. Its gentler mouthfeel and intriguing flavors make it a versatile food wine, good with a wide range of dishes.

Sangiovese

A native of Italy, it can be slightly heavier than pinot noir, but also has a core flavor of cherry pie or wild berry, with layers of earthy tones and a hint of spice. It ranges in style from light red and slightly tart to heavy spice-and-earth wines. Some producers blend in cabernet to give it mainstream appeal, but I love its brick red color and dancing gypsy flavors.

Merlot

A popular red wine with food, merlots range from light fruity styles to heavy, mountain-grown fruit with intense color that makes deep, plummy wines. Softer and fruitier than cabernet and syrah, merlot is a great red wine for sipping and good with a variety of foods.

Zinfandel

The wild child of America, zinfandel, is not widely produced in Europe. Its history is shrouded in confusion, but nothing is confusing about its flavor. It has a standout core of raspberry and black pepper. Styles range from old vine zinfandels with a brick red color and heavy peppercorn, to purple powerhouses with jammy plum flavors and very high alcohol. They are generally served with red meats, grilled vegetables, and pungent cheeses.

Cabernet Sauvignon

Cabernets and syrahs are heavier reds that age gracefully. Cabernet has a luscious mouthfeel with a core flavor of black cherry or plum, and hints of licorice, herbs or violets. The best cabernets are not over-oaked, so you can taste the layers of flavor and enjoy its intriguing bouquet. Its rich, delicious flavors are great for sipping and relaxing, and also excellent with red meats, creamy sauces, and potatoes.

Syrah/Shiraz

Machismo flavors of blueberry, beef, smoke, and licorice characterize this robust red wine—great with hearty cuts of meat, grilled lamb, and blue-veined cheeses. Australian producers call it shiraz.

Other popular red wines include cabernet franc, petite syrah, Mourvedre, grenache, and barbera.

SEPARATING ART AND TECHNIQUE FROM NATURE

A wine made with minimal intervention by the winemaker will feature what I call "vineyard presence." Instead of tasting grapes in the vineyard, it helps to understand that wine grapes are tiny and concentrated, with thick, chewy skins and fat, toasty seeds called pips. The flavor of a wine grape is closely associated with its skin. Wine grapes are distinctly different from the large, juicy, and water-retentive 'table grapes' sold in markets. Ideally, they are small, round, and intensely flavorful, with a low juice-to-skin ratio.

Part of a grape's flavor profile may include woody or spicy components from the skins that are not generally associated with fruit—some white wines have a white pepper nuance, and zinfandel often has a black pepper character. Other flavors intrinsic to certain varieties include minerals, mushroom, leather, and olive.

Once you have learned to recognize the varietal character in general, you're ready to study the effects contributed by winemaking decisions and intervention.

Quality, Ripeness, and Acidity

A certain degree of crisp fruitiness is almost always desirable in a wine, whether white or red. In a white wine, look for the sensation of biting into a fresh, firm, and juicy fruit. In reds, look for the sweet-tart sensation of summer berries and plums.

A wine should convey the same full flavor sensations as summer preserves and jams made from perfectly ripened fruit.

If the wine seems very tart compared to the depth of flavor, it may have been a cool or rainy vintage that prevented the fruit from ripening properly. If a wine tastes raisiny or pruney, the fruit was probably picked too late in the season. Each varietal should have an individualistic flavor. If it does not, the fruit may have come from an over-cropped vineyard. Over cropping dilutes the quality and flavor of the grapes and can result in bland wine. Or, it may be blended from different vineyards for the express purpose of creating a bland, yet pleasant wine.

The winemaker ultimately makes decisions on when to pick, so the quality of the fruit in the glass is the first and primary style decision.

Dry or Sweet

Wine can be completely dry, technically, yet still taste sweet. Higher alcohol levels impart a thicker mouthfeel that you may interpret as 'syrupy' and associate with sweetness. Also, some wines are so robustly fruity that they taste like fruit salad or compotes, and tasters associate the memory of those aromas and flavors with sweetness. Viognier is commonly considered 'sweet' by tasters, and although some certainly are, even a dry viognier can be so powerfully fruity that it will convey a palate memory of sweetness.

Many large productions of chardonnay, in particular, do retain some residual sugar (RS). Residual sugar is not added to the wine—it is the result of leaving some of the natural grape sugars in the wine as opposed to converting all the sugar to alcohol. A little RS in wine can smooth out the flavors and enrich the body. RS is often left in high alcohol reds to balance the wine and prevent a 'hot' mouthfeel.

Residual sugar in a wine is not necessarily a bad thing. Learning to separate perceptions of 'fruit' and 'sweetness' takes practice, and with many wines, it can be difficult even for professionals.

Fat Mouthfeel

A fat mouthfeel refers to a certain viscous, almost oily property in the wine. It's a pleasant experience, also described as luscious or voluptuous. A fat mouthfeel will highlight the deeper flavors of red wines, like roast beef, licorice, and smoke, and create a deep, sensuous experience in white wines, reminiscent of butter and olive oil.

While high alcohol or RS can contribute to a fat mouthfeel, it can also be the result of a higher pH. Levels of pH in wine generally range from 3.5 to 3.7, but many wines can hop as high as 4.2.

Young wines with a heavy mouthfeel are delicious and often multi-layered but are generally designed for early drinking. For wines to cellar, look for bright acids and crisp fruit. Without that bright fruit, wines get flabby quickly. And sometimes, fat wines are better for fireside sipping than serving with food.

Malolactic Conversion

Malolactic conversion (ML) is created by adding malolactic bacteria to a wine after it has completed its primary sugar-to-alcohol fermentation. The ML bacteria convert the sharp malic acids of the grape into creamier, softer, lactic acids. Nearly all reds go through complete ML because they generally taste very bitter without it. For white wines, it becomes a stylistic decision.

ML is more evident in the aroma than in the flavor of white wine. It's a common misconception that ML contributes to a buttery flavor or mouthfeel. That thick, oily butter texture in a white is more likely due to alcohol or sugar. Lactic acids create a butter aroma. To practice identifying it, warm a stick of salted butter to room temperature and study its delicate aroma.

Oak, Vanilla, and Smoke

Not all wines are fermented or stored in oak barrels. Many light, crisp white varietals can be damaged or overwhelmed by time in oak and are at their best when handled in stainless steel. For instance, putting a sauvignon blanc through oak aging or keeping it in stainless would be a winemaker's stylistic decision.

Different types of barrels impart different flavors, ranging from sharp cedar and pine notes to deep, smoky ones. There are so many different flavors and effects that it's a topic of its own—French, American, and Hungarian coopers all have different flavors, as do individual forests and coopers. Even among French barrels, there's a wide variety of flavor. There are also the stylistic decisions of whether to use tight or loose grain; one, two or three-year air-dried wood; light, medium, or heavy toast; and toasted heads.

ASSIGNMENT #3 - DISCERNING SUBTLETY AND MANIPULATION

Equipment for one:

- A glass of wine!

Equipment for six:

- 36 wine glasses and 6 bottles of white wine, all different varietals
- white paper placemats
- notepads and pencils or pens (or use the wine scoring sheet provided)
- bread
- filtered water

Quality, ripeness, and acidity:

For each wine sample, ask yourself:

- Does this wine have a fresh, perfectly ripe character?
- Does it taste under or overripe?
- Does it have a distinct 'varietal character'?

* * *

Dry or sweet

For each wine sample, ask yourself:

- Can I detect clearly identifiable fruit character?
- Does the wine seem sweet?
- If I think the wine is sweet, does that sweetness highlight the fruit, or smother it?

Fat mouthfeel

For each wine sample, ask yourself:

- Does this wine have a fat, unctuous mouthfeel?
- Can I taste more profound and intriguing flavors, beyond the core fruit flavors?
- Would I serve this wine with food, or sip it on its own? Why?

Malolactic conversion

For each wine sample, ask yourself:

- Can I smell lactic acid?
- Is the aroma strong or faint?
- Do I suspect a full or partial ML conversion?
- Do I like/prefer this aroma?

Oak, vanilla, and smoke

For each wine sample, ask yourself:

- Do I detect oak in the aroma?
- How would I describe this particular oak character?
- Is the aroma of oak in balance with the other aromas?
- Is this an aroma I enjoy in this varietal?

COMPONENT DESCRIPTOR KIT

One of the exercises for this super bonus on wine evaluation will involve what the wine industry calls *component descriptor kits*. Although these can be purchased, it is not difficult to make your own. Assembling it will take only a short time, but the ingredients will have to steep for a couple of days.

Equipment:

- 12 quart jars with lids or stretch plastic to cover
- 12 half-pint jars, with lids and screw rings
- fine sieve
- cheesecloth
- small 3M sticky note strips

Ingredients:

- Neutral white wine (a box of Gallo chardonnay or similar wine is fine; you won't be drinking this)

- red food coloring
- 2 cups rocks (gravel or small stones)
- 2 cups green olives, rinsed
- 2 peaches
- 1 box raspberries
- 1 box blackberries
- 1 bunch mint
- 1 mixed bunch of thyme, rosemary, and lavender
- 1 bunch tarragon
- 3 pears
- 3 tablespoons cloves
- 1 box cherries
- 2 tart apples

*Optional/alternates: Meyer lemon, kiwi, plums, peppercorns, alfalfa hay, sage, vanilla extract

Put a pint of wine in each quart jar. Add the rocks to one jar, the olives to another, and the cloves to another jar. Gently crush and twist the bunch of mint and add to a jar, pushing down to cover with wine. Quarter the peaches and add to a quart jar, pushing down to cover with wine. Add the remaining fruit and herbs to separate jars.

Allow to steep for 12 to 48 hours. Pour off a little of the pear infusion and smell. When the pear and apple infusions are strong enough to identify, the others will be ready as well. Clean the half-pint jars and rinse thoroughly. Make sure they do not smell like cardboard or soap. Strain each infusion by pouring through a fine sieve lined with a layer of cheesecloth. Pour each infusion into a clean half-pint jar. Color the "red" aromas (raspberries, blackberries, cherries, mint, tarragon, and cloves) with red food coloring by adding one drop at a time and stir until the wine turns ruby red. Olives and herbs may be left white or colored red as they can apply to both. Seal the jars until ready to use, and label with sticky notes.

ASSIGNMENT #4 - USING YOUR COMPONENT DESCRIPTOR KIT

Use your infusions to familiarize yourself with characteristic individual wine aromas. By practicing blind, the exercise of identifying a unique aroma will train your mind to scroll back through your sensory experiences for a match. With experience and practice, you can train yourself to recognize individual aromatic components in a glass of wine.

The following exercises and practice sessions are, as always, more enlightening and fun when shared with friends, but you can do them solo as well.

Equipment for one:

- A glass of wine!

Equipment for six:

- 36 wine glasses and 6 bottles of white wine, all different varietals
- white paper placemats

- notepads and pencils or pens (or use the wine scoring sheet provided)
- bread
- filtered water

Exercise #1

Arrange the jars on a table or flat surface. Use place cards by each jar to identify the aroma. Inhale each aroma and look away or close your eyes, committing the aroma to memory. Visualizing the scent often helps. "See" the fruit, herb, or spice in your mind, and "feel" it in your hand.

Exercise #2

Rearrange the scent jars and close or overturn the place cards. Try to recognize and identify each scent.

Again, a visual organization may help. Imagine yourself cruising the aisles of a grocery store or outdoor market looking for the source of the aroma. Remember to peruse your mental garden, pantry, and spice rack for surprising and elusive aromas. Try to visualize what the scent would be if you opened your eyes and were holding it in your hand.

Scents will be interpreted differently by everyone. Here are some common variations:

- *gravel, mineral* = limestone, saltiness, earth
- *peaches* = apricots, stone fruit
- *herbs* = herbs de Provence, sage, marjoram, cut grass

- *tarragon* = licorice, anise, fennel
- *cloves* = nutmeg, exotic spice

Exercise #3

Evaluate the aromas of a white wine and a red wine. Try to determine if the scents in your kit are present or absent.

About The Instructor:

Mary Baker (Rebel Rose) is the owner of Dover Canyon Winery, a small artisanal producer in Paso Robles, California. She has taught college-sponsored courses in wine appreciation and frequently speaks on wine appreciation and food-and-wine pairing. Thirteen years in wine hospitality and winery business management include stints as the first tasting room manager for Wild Horse Winery, and later the business manager for Justin Winery.

As one of the original moderators on AOL's Food and Drink Network, Mary hosted monthly online winemaker chats. From 2002 to 2004, she served as a director on the board of the local vintners' association, representing the Paso Robles appellation, entertaining international visitors, and speaking at local wine festivals and seminars. She was also chairman of the 2004 Paso Robles Zinfandel Festival, an annual wine festival featuring a grand tasting, live and silent auctions, press events, artist receptions, and open house events at over 80 wineries.

In her spare time, she writes and plants vegetables and flowers, many of which promptly die.

She is the author of *Fresh From Dover Canyon: Easy Elegant Recipes from Dover Canyon Winery*, available on Amazon.com.

We would like to thank Mary for allowing us to offer you this course on wine tasting as a bonus to this winemaking manual! You might as learn how to properly taste (and enjoy your wine), given all of the efforts you've put into making it!

To learn more about the Dover Canyon Winery, please visit:

www.DoverCanyon.com

APPENDIX E: GUIDE ON HOW TO PROPERLY PRESENT YOUR WINE

I mpress your friends and family by following these simple six steps when presenting them with a bottle of wine:

Step 1 – **Present the bottle of wine to the person who brought the bottle,** making sure that the label is facing them.

Step 2 – **Holding the bottle with one hand use the other hand to remove the shrink** (the wrap at the top of the bottle covering the cork) using a bartender's corkscrew and be sure not to turn the bottle at all while you are doing this (this may take a bit of practice).

Note: This whole bottle opening "maneuver" should be done while holding the bottle in the air and not done by placing the bottle on the table by the guest.

. . .

Step 3 – **Remove the cork by pushing the screw from the bottle opener on an angle** down the side of the neck of the bottle into the cork. Then begin turning the handle of the corkscrew clockwise so that the screw enters the cork.

Step 4 - **Once the corkscrew is approximately ¾ of the way into the cork, place the lever of the corkscrew on the lip of the bottle.** Push up slowly on the opposite end of the corkscrew handle to remove the cork making sure that the cork doesn't come out with a "pop."

Remember: Try not to turn the bottle as you are turning the corkscrew.

Step 5 – **Remove the cork from the corkscrew and hand it to the guest you were presenting the bottle** so that they can examine it to determine whether or not the bottle has been stored correctly. The main thing that they will look for is a nice moist cork and not a cork that is crumbly or dried out.

Step 6 – **Pour a small amount of wine into the glass of the person who brought it** to allow them to taste it to ensure that it meets with their approval. Once they have approved the wine, pour an appropriate amount into the other guest's glasses at the table (beginning with the ladies) finishing off with the original person who brought the wine.

A bottle of wine should serve approximately 4-5 people, and you should try to ensure that everyone at the table has an equal amount of wine in their glass.

APPENDIX F: WINE/LIQUOR RECIPES & TUTORIALS

One thing I suggested earlier was making wine from fresh fruit. If you're interested in giving this a whirl, here are a bunch of recipes that I found for you that will help get you on your way!

FRESH FRUIT WINES:

Method 1 makes wines of the heaver type; their flavors are more pronounced, and their color more full than those produced by *method 2.*

Those wishing for lighter wines more suitable for serving with meals should use *method 2.* The main difference in the two methods is that we ferment the fruit pulp itself in *method 1,* and the juice only in *method 2.*

When fermenting the pulp, we must get far more from our fruits. But we do not want too much in a light wine; otherwise, the subtle difference between a heavier wine and the popular lighter wines is lost.

The short pulp ferment of *method 1* ensures that we get all of the flavors from our fruits in the right proportion.

The best method to use for each type of fruit is given with each recipe. You should take into account that varying amounts of fruit and sugar with the use of the proper method will produce distinctly different types of wine.

METHOD 1

Crush the fruit by hand in a polythene pail and pour on one quart of boiled water that has cooled. Mix well. Crush one Campden tablet and dissolve the powder in about half an egg cupful of warm water and mix this with the fruit pulp.

Leave the mixture for one or two hours. A little bleaching will take place, but this is nothing to worry about. Then, take one-third of the sugar to be used and boil this for one minute in three pints of water.

Allow this syrup to cool and then stir into the pulp. Then add the yeast (or nucleus) and ferment for seven days. After seven days, strain the pulp through fine muslin or other similar material and wring out as dry as you can. Put the strained wine into a gallon jar and throw the pulp away. Then boil another one-third of the sugar in one pint of water for one minute, and when this has cooled, add it to the rest. Plug the neck of the jar with cotton wool or fit a fermentation lock and continue to ferment in a warm place for a further ten days.

At this stage, if you don't have a spare jar, pour the wine into a polythene pail leaving as much of the deposit in the jar as you can. Clean out the jar, sterilize it and return the wine to this. The remaining one-third of the sugar may now be boiled for one minute in the remaining pint of water. When this has cooled, add it to the rest. Refit the lock or plug the neck of the jar with fresh cotton wool. After this, the wine should be left in a warm place until all fermentation has ceased.

NOTE: If there is not quite enough space for all of this last lot of syrup, put the remainder in a sterilized screw-top bottle and store for a few days in a cool place. The syrup may be added when fermentation has reduced the level of the liquid in the jar. If you have to do this, don't forget to refit the lock.

METHOD 2

Crush the fruit in a polythene pail and add one quart of boiled water that has cooled. Mix well. Crush one Campden tablet and dissolve the powder in about half an egg cupful of warm water and mix this with the fruit pulp. Leave the mixture in a cool place for twenty-four hours, stirring twice during that time. Strain through fine muslin or other similar material and squeeze gently but not too hard. Discard the fruit pulp.

Then boil one-third of the sugar in half a gallon of water for one minute and allow it to cool. Mix this with the juice and return the lot to the polythene pail. Then add the yeast (or nucleus), and ferment for ten days. Then, pour the wine into a gallon jar leaving as much of the deposit behind as you can. Boil another one-third of the sugar in half a pint of water for one minute, and when it is cool, add it to the rest.

Plug the neck of the jar with cotton wool or fit a fermentation lock and ferment in a warm place for fourteen days.

After this, boil the remaining sugar in the remaining half-pint of water for one minute, and when cool, add it to the rest. Refit the lock or plug the neck of the jar with fresh cotton wool and leave in a warm place until all fermentation has ceased. The recipes are designed to make one gallon of wine. If two gallons are being made at once twice, the amount of each ingredient must be used (including Campden tablets), and the sugar and water added in double quantities. This principle applies where three or four gallons are being made, and it is easy enough to work out. Just to be sure that mistakes do not occur when adding the syrup-sugar and water-stick a label on the jar and note on this, the amount added.

Readers will be quick to appreciate that certain fruits are more suitable than others for making certain types of wine. It would be as hopeless to try to make port from rhubarb as it would be to try to grow potatoes on a pear tree, and I think it is in this respect that many people go astray. They make wines from the cheapest and most readily available fruits, but they do not give the slightest thought to what the result will be or whether they will like it or not.

Before you begin decide on the type of wine you are most likely to prefer and then use the fruit and the method which will make this type of wine. Elderberries make an excellent port-style wine so that from this lowly wild fruit, we may obtain not only a full-bodied port-style wine but also a Burgundy style, a claret, and others according to the whim of the operator.

Blackberries make similar wines, as do certain varieties of plums, damsons, and black currants. The juice from lighter-colored fruit such as raspberries, loganberries, red and white currants, and others make excellent table wines. Every recipe is preceded by the type or style of wine that can be expected from each recipe. I say 'expected' because to guarantee that the wine will be identical to the one expected would be unwise. Still, only because the amounts of sugar and acid present in the fruits vary from season to season -indeed, they vary with the type of tree, soil, situation, and with the sort of summer we have had while the fruits have been growing. A hot summer produces fruits containing more sugar and less acid than a wet sunless summer when the effect is the reverse.

Each recipe includes the name of the best yeast to use. Merely sprinkle it over the surface of the 'must' at the time given in the method you are using.

A final word. Make sure all fruits are ripe, which is far more critical than most people imagine. Half-ripe fruits or those with green patches on them should be discarded as it needs only one or two of these to give a gallon of wine an acid bite. Fully ripe fruit is essential if we hope to make the best wine.

When we have decided that our garden fruits are ripe enough or those you have your eye on in the hedgerows, leave them for another three or four days before gathering.

RECIPES 1 - 32 (BERRY WINES)

1. BLACKBERRY WINE (Port Style):

4lb. blackberries, 4lb. sugar (or 5lb. invert), 7pts. water, port yeast, nutrient.

Use method 1. Ferment the pulp.

2. BLACKBERRY AND ELDERBERRY WINE (Port Style):

2 1/2lb. elderberries, 2 1/2lb. blackberries, 7pts. water,

3 1/2lb. sugar (or 4lb. invert), port yeast, nutrient.

Use method 1. Ferment the pulp after crushing and mixing.

3. BLACKBERRY WINE (Burgundy Style):

4-5lb. blackberries, 3 3/8lb. sugar (or 4lb. invert), burgundy yeast, nutrient, 7pts water.

Use method 1. Ferment the pulp.

4. BLACKBERRY WINE (Beaujolais Style):

4 1/2lb. blackberries, 2 1/2lb. sugar (or 3lb. 2oz. invert), burgundy yeast, nutrient, 7pts. water. Method 1 was used. The wine was, of course, dry.

5. BLACKBERRY WINE (Light Table Wine):

3lb. blackberries, 3lb. sugar (3 3/4lb. invert), 7pts. water, burgundy yeast, nutrient.

Use method 2. Ferment the diluted juice.

6. BLACKCURRANT WINE (Port Style):

4lb. blackcurrants, 1lb. raisins, 3lb. sugar (or 3 3/4lb. invert), port yeast, nutrient.

Use method 1. Ferment the pulp with the raisins.

7. BLACKCURRANT WINE (Port Style):

4lb. blackcurrants, 7pts. water, 3 1/2lb. sugar (or 4lb. invert), port yeast, nutrient.

Use method 1. Ferment the pulp.

8. BLACKCURRANT CLARET:

4lb. blackcurrants, 2 1/2lb. sugar 3lwater, all-purpose wine yeast

Use method 2. Ferment the diluted juice.

9. BLACKCURRANT WINE (A Light, Sweet Wine):

3 3/4lb. blackcurrants, 3 1/2lb. sugar (or 7pts. water, all-purpose wine yeast, nutrient.

Use method 2. Ferment the diluted juice.

10. CHERRY WINE (A Delightful Sweet Wine):

8lb. black cherries, 7pts. water, 3 1/2lb. invert), all-purpose wine yeast or Bordeaux nutrient.

Use method 1 Weight with stones and ferment the pulp.

11. CHERRY WINE (A Light Dry Wine):

8lb. black cherries, 7pts. water, 2 1/2lb. sugar (or 3

1/4lb. invert), sherry yeast is best, all-purpose wine yeast, nutrient.

Use method 2. Ferment the strained diluted juice.

12. REDCURRANT WINE (Light Table Wine):

3lb. red currants, 7pts. water, 3lb. sugar, (or 3 3/ invert), all-purpose wine yeast, nutrient

Use method 2. Ferment the strained dilute.

13. REDCURRANT WINE (A Light Medium-Sweet Wine):

4lb. red currants, 7pts. water, 3 1/2lb. sugar (or 4 invert), all-purpose wine yeast, nutrient.

Use method 2. Ferment the strained diluted juice.

14. DAMSON WINE (Port Style):

8lb. damsons, 7pts. water, 4lb. sugar, (or 5lb. inv) port yeast, nutrient.

Use method 1. Weight with the stones and ferment the pulp.

15. DAMSON WINE:

Suitable for making into Damson Gin-See 'Recent Experiments'. 5lb. damsons,

7pts. water, 3lb. sugar (or 3 3/4lb. invert), all-purpose wine yeast, nutrient.

Use method 1. Weight with the stones. Ferment the pulp.

16. DAMSON AND ELDERBERRY WINE (Port Style):

3lb. damsons, 1 1/2lb. elderberries, 3 1/2lb. sugar (or 4lb. invert), port yeast, nutrient, 7pts. water

Use method 1. Ferment the pulp.

17. DAMSON AND DRIED PRUNE WINE (Burgundy Style):

Prunes should be soaked overnight and the prunes added in the crushed state to the crushed

4lb. damsons, 2lb. dried prunes, 7pts. water, 3lb. sugar (or 3lb. invert), 7pts. e diluted juice. : 4lb. invert), sugar (or 4lb. yeast,

18. RASPBERRY WINE (Light, Dry):

4lb. raspberries, 2 1/2lb. sugar, (or 3lb. 2oz. invert),

7pts. water, sherry yeast or all-purpose wine yeast, nutrient.

Use method 2. Ferment the strained diluted juice.

19. RASPBERRY WINE (Sweet Dessert):

4 lbs. raspberries, 1lb. raisins, 7pts. water, 3 1/2lb. sugar, (or 4lb. invert),

all-purpose wine yeast and nutrient. Use method 2.

Ferment the strained diluted juice but with the chopped raisins for the first seven days.

20. ELDERBERRY WINE (Port Style):

4lb. elderberries, 7pts. water, 4lb. sugar (or 5lb. invert), port yeast, nutrient.

Use method 1. Ferment the crushed pulp.

21. ELDERBERRY WINE (Medium Dry): invert),

3 1/2lb. elderberries, 3lb. sugar (or 3 3/4lb. invert) 7 pts water, sherry yeast

or all-purpose wine yeast, nutrient.

Use method 2. Ferment the strained diluted juice.

22. ELDERBERRY CLARET (Dry, of course):

3lb. elderberries, 2 1/2lb. sugar (or 3lb invert), 7pts. water, sherry yeast or all-purpose

Use method 2. Ferment the strained diluted juice.

23. PLUM WINE (Burgundy Style):

8lb. plums, any fully ripe variety is suitable, 7pts. water,

3lb. sugar (or 3 3/4lb. invert), burgundy yeast, nutrient.

Use method 1. Weight with the stones and ferment the crushed pulp.

24. PLUM WINE (Port Style):

Dark red, fully ripe fruits must be used. 10lb. plums, 7pts. water, 3 1/2lb. sugar

(or 4lb. invert), port yeast, nutrient. Weight with the stones.

Use method 1. Ferment the crushed pulp.

25. RHUBARB WINE:

This wine is best made on the dry side and used as an appetizer. If you try to make it sweet, it would have to be slightly too sweet. Four pounds of sugar will make it a medium-sweet wine, but even this will not reduce the acidity, which gives this wine its character, which, unfortunately, is causing it to lose its popularity. It is possible to remove the acid by using precipitated chalk, but this is hard for beginners and a practice which, in any case, alters the whole flavor of the resulting wine.

5lb. rhubarb, 3lb. sugar (or 3 3/4lb. invert), 7pts. water, sherry yeast or all-purpose wine yeast, nutrient. Crush the rhubarb with a rolling pin, starting in the middle of each stick. Soak for five days in three pints of water (boiled), and in which one Campden tablet has been dissolved. Then strain, wring out, dry and warm just enough to dissolve half of the sugar.

Having done this, ferment for ten days and then proceed as you would with any other recipe here, adding the rest of the sugar and water in stages.

26. LOGANBERRY WINE:

3 to 4lb. loganberries, 3lb. sugar (or 3 ¾lb. invert),

burgundy yeast, nutrient, 7 pts water.

Use method 1. Ferment the crushed pulp.

27. GOOSEBERRY WINE (Table Wine):

6lb. gooseberries, 3.5 lb. sugar (or 4 ¼lb. invert),

7pts. water, tokay yeast or all-purpose wine yeast, nutrient.

Use method 1. But ferment pulp for three days.

28. GOOSEBERRY WINE (Sherry Style):

The best gooseberries for this wine are those that have been left on the bushes to turn red or yellow, according to variety. They should be firm but soft and, at the same time, not damaged. Any damaged ones and any with a suggestion of mold or mildew on them must be discarded.

For a dry sherry style, use 2 1/2lb. sugar, for a medium-dry use 3lb., and for a medium sweet use 3 1/2lb., or the corresponding amounts of invert sugar. 5lb. gooseberries, 7pts. water, sugar (as above), sherry yeast or all-purpose wine yeast, nutrient. Use method 1. But ferment the pulp for five days only

29. WHORTLEBERRY WINE (Burgundy Style):

Whortleberries are a small wild fruit that many people come to the country to pick; they make excellent jams and jellies - and outstanding wines, otherwise known as 'herts.'

6pts whortleberries, 7pts. water, 3lb. sugar (or 3 3/4lb. invert), burgundy yeast, nutrient.

Use method 1. Ferment the pulp.

30. WHORTLEBERRY WINE (Port Style):

8pts. whortleberries, 7pts. water, 4lb. sugar (or 5lb. invert), port yeast, nutrient.

Use method 1. Ferment the pulp.

31. WHORTLEBERRY WINE (Table Wine):

5pts. whortleberries, 7pts. water, 2 1/2lb/ sugar (or 3lb. 2oz. invert), all-purpose wine yeast, nutrient.

Use method 2. Ferment the strained diluted juice.

32. SLOE WINE:

Sloes make a delightful wine, which is very popular with those living in the country and is particularly suitable for turning into sloe gin. Not more than 4lb. should be used owing to their astringency. 4lb. sloes, 3lb. sugar (or 3 3/4lb invert), 7pts. water. All-purpose wine yeast, nutrient. Use method 1. But ferment pulp for three days only.

EXTRACT TUTORIAL:

This lesson will show you how easily the flavor of world-famous liqueurs and other commercial products may be added with the minimum of utensils and labor; indeed, this is probably, if not decidedly, the simplest, the least troublesome and the most rewarding of all adventures in winemaking.

In what is known as T'Noirot Extracts, we have a readily prepared ingredient and, as will be seen in the recipes, no preparation is needed, the stuff is ready to use.

When making these wines, please use good quality yeast and nutrient, for the results obtained in this way will surpass any you can hope to achieve by using bakers' yeast and no nutrient.

It will be seen in the recipes that Invert sugar has been included because this gives the best results here. Invert sugar contains a little acid, and this is essential in wine-making as we have already seen. If you use household sugar, you will have to add the juice of one lemon or a one-eighth ounce of citric acid to give just the tiny amount of acid required.

When adding the extract to the prepared syrup (sugar-water), make sure you get all of it out of the bottles.

When deciding which extract to use, you must first decide on which you are likely to prefer (unless you know in advance and from experience that you like Vermouth or Kirsh or cherry brandy) and then choose that one. In this way, you will make a wine that might disappoint you-after all; not all tastes are the same.

VERY IMPORTANT: The method we shall be using calls for adding these very highly concentrated flavorings to a very small amount of liquid, to begin with.

The flavor will be very, very strong, so do not sample it, and the odor given off might strike people as not quite pleasant. It is quite natural, so do not be put off using them because of this. And don't take a 'sniff' of the wine during the early stages, for the same reason.

T'NOIROT EXTRACTS AND WHAT THEY ARE MADE OF:

The following list contains the names of most of the T'Noirot Extracts that we shall be using in this Lesson, and beside each appears details of their contents. The extracts are scientifically blended to give flavors identical to the world-famous liqueurs of the same names. Thus you are assured of the real thing and not a synthetic substitute.

These flavorings are highly concentrated and should not, therefore, be judged by their odor. Anyone smelling the raw, undiluted material or sampling the wines made from the extracts is likely to imagine that something is not quite right.

Do not pay any attention to the strength or pungency of the odor and do not sample any wines being made from the extract until fermentation has almost ceased. Even at this stage, it is not wise to try to judge the wine. Wait, I implore you until fermentation has ceased altogether, and the wine has been clear for at least a month. As with all other wines, the flavor improves immensely with age.

And let me just add that the oil of juniper mentioned in other parts of this book is an extract of juniper berries - juniper being an ornamental shrub grown a good deal in this country.

LIQUEUR GREEN CONVENT / LIQUEUR YELLOW CONVENT

Both distilled from plants growing in the high mountain regions. These two established the now world-wide reputation of T'Noirot.

CURACAO, RED / CURACAO, WHITE

Two liqueurs of Dutch origin distilled from small green oranges.

CHERRY BRANDY

It is made from unfermented cherries.

DANZIG

A liqueur of German origin.

KUMMEL

Of continental origin, it is extracted from the caraway seed. Wine made from this extract would act as a stimulant of the digestive organs.

MIRABELLE

It is distilled from the famous Lorraine plum.

PRUNELLE

It is distilled from the wild plum.

Many of the extracts contain blends of bitter and aromatic plants - Vermouth being a good example of this. We are all well aware of the delicate flavors of the French and Italian Vermouths and will thus be enabled to appreciate the value of all the T'Noirot Extracts, for they bring us something unique when it comes to making wines from them.

As will be seen in the recipes, it is advised carrying out the entire fermentation in the gallon jar. Still, if you would prefer to ferment for the first ten days in a polythene pail, by all means, do so, but make certain, it is covered as directed earlier. If you do this, give the liquor a good stir before putting it into the jar; otherwise, some of the deposit and a lot of flavoring may be lost. Do not on any account divide the liquor, say, into two half-gallon lots because half-gallon jars happen to be available. Keep it as one until all fermentation has ceased. When this has happened, the clearer wine may be siphoned off the deposit into another jar and put away to clear. When clear, it should be bottled.

CHERRY BRANDY WINE

6 bottles of cherry brandy extract, 3 lb. sugar (or 3 ¾ invert), 1 gal. water, yeast, and nutrient.

Boil one-third of the sugar in half a gallon of water for two minutes, allow to cool, and pour into the gallon jar. Then add the extract, yeast, and nutrient.

Cover as directed of fit fermentation lock and ferment in a warm place for ten days. Then boil another third of the sugar in a further quart of water for two minutes, and when cool, add this to the rest. Cover again as before or refit the lock and continue to ferment in a warm place for a further fourteen days. After this, boil the rest of the sugar in the remaining quart of water as before, and when cool, add the rest. Cover again or refit the lock and leave in a cool place until all fermentation has ceased.

VERMOUTH (ITALIAN)

6 bottles of Italian Vermouth extract, 3 lb. sugar (or 3 3/4 lb. invert), yeast and nutrient.

Boil one-third of the sugar in a half-gallon of water for two minutes. Allow to cool and pour into a gallon jar. Then add the extract, yeast, and nutrient. Cover as directed or fit fermentation lock and ferment in a warm place for ten days. The boil another one-third of the sugar in a further quart of water, and when this is cool, add it to the rest. Cover again or refit the lock and continue to ferment in a warm place for a further fourteen days. After this, boil the remaining sugar in the remaining quart of water as before, then add to the rest. Cover again or refit the lock and leave in a warm place until all fermentation has ceased.

VERMOUTH (FRENCH)

6 bottles of French Vermouth extract, 3 1/4 lb. sugar (or 4 lb. invert), 1 gal. water, yeast nutrient.

Boil one-third of the sugar in half a gallon of water for two minutes and when cool pour into a gallon jar. Then add the extract, yeast, and nutrient. Cover as directed or fit fermentation lock and ferment in a warm place for ten days. Then boil another one-one third of the sugar in a quart of water for two minutes, and when cool, add this to the rest. Allow to ferment in a warm place for a further fourteen days.

After this, boil the remaining water and sugar as before and when cool add to the rest. Cover again or refit the lock and continue to ferment in a warm place until all fermentation has ceased.

CREAM OF APRICOT WINE

5 bottles of apricot extract, 3 lb. sugar, (or 3 3/4 lb. invert), 1 gal. water, yeast, and nutrient.

Boil one-third of the sugar in half a gallon of water for two minutes, allow to cool, and pour into a gallon jar. Then add the extract, yeast, and nutrient. Cover as directed or fit fermentation lock and ferment in a warm place for ten days. Then boil another third of the sugar in a quart of the water for two minutes, and when this is cool, add it to the rest. Cover again as directed or refit fermentation lock and continue to ferment in a warm place for a further fourteen days. After this, boil the rest of the sugar in the remaining water as before and when cool add to the rest. Cover again or refit lock and continue to ferment in a warm place until all fermentation has ceased.

CREAM OF PEACH WINE

6 bottles of cream of peach, 3 lb. sugar (or 3 3/4 lb. invert), 1 gal. water, yeast, and nutrient.

Boil one-third of the sugar in half-gallon of water for two minutes and when cool pour into a gallon-size glass jar. Then add the extract, yeast, and nutrient. Cover as directed or fit fermentation lock and ferment in a warm place for ten days.

Then boil another one-third of the sugar in a quart of water, and when cool, add this to the rest. Cover again as directed or refit the lock and continue to ferment in a warm place for a further fourteen days.

After this, boil the rest of the sugar in the remaining water as before and when cool add to the rest. Cover again as directed or refit the lock and continue to ferment in a warm place until all fermentation has ceased.

SLOE GIN WINE

6 bottles of sloe gin extract, 3 lb. sugar (or 3 3/4 lb. invert), 1 gal. water, yeast, and nutrient.

Boil one-third of the sugar in a half-gallon of water for two minutes and when cool pour into a gallon jar. Then add the extract, yeast, and nutrient. Cover as directed or fit fermentation lock and ferment in a warm place for ten days. Then boil another one-third of the sugar in a quart of water as before, and when this is cool, add to the rest. Cover again or refit lock and continue to ferment in a warm place for a further fourteen days. Then boil the rest of the sugar in the remaining water as before and when cool add to the rest. Cover again, refit the lock and continue to ferment in a warm place until all fermentation has ceased.

RATAFIA WINE

6 bottles of Ratafia extract, 3 lb. sugar (or 3 3/4 lb. invert), 1 gal. water, yeast, and nutrient.

Boil one-third of the sugar in a half-gallon of water for two minutes and when cool pour into a gallon glass jar. Then add the extract, yeast, and nutrient. Cover as directed or fit fermentation lock and ferment in a warm place for ten days. The boil another one-third of the sugar in a quart of water as before, and when this is cool, add it to the rest. Cover again or refit lock and continue to ferment in a warm place for a further fourteen days.

After this, boil the rest of the sugar in the remaining water as before and when cool add to the rest. Cover again as directed or fit fermentation lock and continue to ferment in a warm place until all fermentation has ceased.

KIRSCH WINE

6 bottles of Kirsch extract, 3 lb. sugar (or 3 3/4 lb. invert), 1 gal. water, yeast, and nutrient.

Boil one-third of the sugar in half a gallon of water for two minutes and when cool pour into a gallon glass jar. Then add the extract, yeast, and nutrient. Cover as directed or fit fermentation lock and ferment in a warm place for ten days. Then boil another one-third of the sugar in a quart of water as before, and when this is cool, add it to the rest. Cover as directed or refit lock and continue to ferment in a warm place for a further fourteen days. After this, boil the remaining sugar in the rest of the water as before and when cool add to the rest. Cover again as directed or refit the lock and continue to ferment in a warm place until all fermentation has ceased.

MIRABELLE WINE

6 bottles of Mirabelle extract, 3 lb. sugar (or 3 3/4 lb. invert), 1 gal. water, yeast, and nutrient.

Boil one-third of the sugar in a half-gallon of water for two minutes and when cool pour into a gallon glass jar. Then add the extract, yeast, and nutrient. Cover as directed or fit fermentation lock and ferment in a warm place for ten days. The boil another one-third of the sugar in a quart of water as before and when it is cool add to the rest. Cover again or refit the lock and ferment in a warm place for another fourteen days. After this, boil the remaining sugar in the rest of the water as before and when cool add to the rest.

Cover again as directed or refit the lock and continue to ferment in a warm place until all fermentation has ceased.

PRUNELLE WINE

6 bottles of Prunelle extract, 3 lb. sugar, (or 3 ¾ invert), 1 gal. water, yeast, and nutrient.

Boil one-third of the sugar in half a gallon of water for two minutes and when cool pour into a gallon jar. Then add the extract, yeast, and nutrient. Cover as directed or fit fermentation lock and ferment in a warm place for ten days. Then boil another one-third of the sugar in a quart of water as before, and when this is cool, add it to the rest. Cover again or refit the lock and continue to ferment in a warm place for a further fourteen days. After this, boil the remaining sugar in the rest of the water as before and when cool add to the rest. Cover again or refit the lock and continue to ferment in a warm place until all fermentation has ceased.

MARASQUIN WINE

6 bottles of Marassquin extract, 3 lb. sugar (or 3 ¾ lb. invert), 1 gal. water, yeast, and nutrient.

Boil one-third of sugar in a half-gallon of water for two minutes and when cool pour into a gallon glass jar. Then pour in the extract, yeast, and nutrient.

Cover as directed or fit fermentation lock and ferment in a warm place for ten days. Then boil another one-third of the sugar in a quart of water for two minutes, and when cool, add this to the rest. Cover again or refit lock and continue to ferment in a warm place for another fourteen days.

After this, boil the remaining sugar in the rest of the water as before and when cool add to the rest. Cover again or refit the lock and continue to ferment in a warm place until all fermentation has ceased.

MANDARINE WINE

6 bottles of Mandarine extract, 3 lb. sugar (or 3 3/4 lb. invert), a gal. water, yeast, and nutrient.

Boil one-third of sugar in a gallon of water for two minutes and when cool pour into a gallon glass jar. Then add the extract, yeast, and nutrient. Cover as directed or fit fermentation lock and ferment in a warm place for ten days. Then boil another one-third of the sugar in a quart of water as before, and when cool, add this to the rest. Cover again or refit lock and continue to ferment in a warm place for a further fourteen days.

After this, boil the remaining sugar in the rest of the water as before and when cool add to the rest. Cover again or refit the lock and continue to ferment in a warm place until all fermentation has ceased.

GREEN CONVENT WINE

5 bottles of Green Convent extract, 3 lb. sugar (or 3 ¾ lb. invert), 1 gal. water, yeast, and nutrient.

Boil one-third of the sugar in half a gallon of water for two minutes and when cool pour into a gallon glass jar. Then add the extract, yeast, and nutrient. Cover as directed or fit fermentation lock and ferment in a warm place for ten days. Then boil another one-third of the sugar in a quart of water as before, and when cool, add this to the rest.

Cover again and continue to ferment for another fourteen days.

After this, boil the remaining sugar in the rest of the water as before and when cool add to the rest. Cover again and continue to ferment until all fermentation has ceased.

YELLOW CONVENT WINE

5 bottles of Yellow Convent extract, 3 lb. sugar (or 3 3/4 lb. invert), 1 gal. water, yeast, and nutrient.

Boil one-third of the sugar in half a gallon of water for two minutes and when cool pour into a gallon glass jar. Then pour in the extract, yeast, and nutrient. Cover and ferment for ten days. Then boil another one-third of the sugar, and when cool, add it to the rest. Cover again and continue to ferment in a warm place for another fourteen days.

Then boil the remaining sugar in the rest of the water as before and when cool add to the rest. Cover again and ferment in a warm place until all fermentation has ceased.

REVERENDINE WINE

6 bottles of Reverendine extract, 3 lb. sugar (or 3 ¾ lb. invert), 1 gal. water, yeast nutrient.

Boil one-third of the sugar in half a gallon of water for two minutes and when cool pour into a gallon glass jar. Then pour in the extract, yeast, and nutrient. Cover and ferment in a warm place for ten days. Then boil another one-third of the sugar as before, and when cool, add it to the rest. Cover again and continue to ferment in a warm place for a further fourteen days. After this, boil the remaining sugar in the rest of the water as before, and when cool, add it to the rest. Cover again and continue to ferment in a warm place until all fermentation has ceased.

RED CURACAO WINE

6 bottles of Red Curacao extract, 3 lb. sugar, (or 3 ¾ lb. invert), 1 gal. water, yeast, and nutrient.

Boil one-third of the sugar in half a gallon of water for two minutes and when cool pour into a glass jar. Then add the extract, yeast, and nutrient. Cover and ferment in a warm place for ten days. Then boil another one-third of the sugar as before, and when cool, add it to the rest. Cover again and ferment in a warm place for another fourteen days. After this, boil the remaining sugar in the rest of the water as before, and when cool, add it to the rest. Cover again and continue to ferment until all fermentation has ceased.

WHITE CURACAO WINE

6 bottles of White Curacao extract, 3 lb. sugar (or 3 ¾ lb. invert) 1 gal. water, yeast, and nutrient.

Boil one-third of the sugar in half a gallon of water, and when this is cool, pour into a gallon glass jar. Then pour in the extract, and add the yeast and nutrient. Cover the jar and ferment in a warm place for ten days. Then boil another one-third of the sugar in a quart of water as before and when cool add to the rest. Cover again and continue to ferment for another fourteen days.

After this, boil the remaining sugar in the rest of the water as before and when cool add to the rest. Cover again and ferment in a warm place until all fermentation has ceased.

KUMMEL WINE

6 bottles of Kummel extract, 3 lb. sugar (or 3 3/4 lb.invert), 1 gal. water, yeast, and nutrient.

Boil one-third of the sugar in half a gallon of water for two minutes and when cool pour into a gallon glass bottle. Then add the extract, yeast, and nutrient.

Cover and fermentation for ten days. Then boil another one-third of the sugar in a quart of water as before, and when this is cool, add it to the rest. Cover again and ferment in a warm place for another fourteen days. After this, boil the remaining sugar in the rest of the water as before, and when cool, add it to the rest. Cover again and continue to ferment in a warm place until all fermentation has ceased.

DANZIG WINE

6 bottles of Danzig extract, 3 lb. sugar (or 3 3/4 lb. invert), 1 gal. water, yeast, and nutrient.

Boil one-third of the sugar in half a gallon of water for two minutes and when cool pour into a gallon glass jar. Then pour in the extract, yeast, and nutrient.

Cover and ferment in a warm place for ten days. Then boil another one-third of the sugar in a quart of water as before, and when cool, add this to the rest. Cover again and continue to ferment in a warm place for another fourteen days.

After this, boil the remaining sugar in the rest of the water as before, and when it is cool, add it to the rest. Cover again and ferment in a warm place until all fermentation has ceased.

EAU-DE-VIE WINE

6 bottles of extract of Eau-de-Vie, 3 lb. sugar (or 3 3/4lb. invert), 1 gal. water, yeast, and nutrient.

Boil one-third of the sugar in half a gallon of water for two minutes and when cool pour into a gallon glass jar. Then add extract, yeast, and nutrient.

Cover as directed and ferment in a warm place for ten days. Then boil another one-third of the sugar in a quart of water as before, and when cool, add this to the rest. Cover again and ferment in a warm place for another fourteen days. After this, boil the remaining sugar in the rest of the water as before and when cool add to the rest. Cover again as directed and continue to ferment in a warm place until all fermentation has ceased.

Wines From Citrus Fruits:

ORANGE WINE

This is a delightful wine that develops a flavor that can readily be likened to an orange-flavored whiskey. 12 large oranges, or their equivalent, 4 lb. sugar, ½ oz. yeast, 1 gal. water, nutrient. Drop the whole oranges into boiling water, and push each one under the surface. Then take them out and throw the water away. Cut the oranges into small pieces and pour over them half a gallon of boiled water that has cooled. Cover well, and leave to soak for forty-eight hours, crushing and pressing the peel between the fingers to extract the oil, which gives a very special flavor. Then boil half the sugar in a quart of water for two minutes, and when cooled, add this to the orange pulp. Then add the yeast and nutrient. Ferment this in a warm place for five days.

Then crush, strain through fine muslin or other suitable material, and wring out dry. Discard the pulp and return the fermenting liquor to the fermenting vessel and allow it to ferment for a further ten days. Carefully pour off into a gallon jar, leaving as much of the deposit behind as you can. Then boil the rest of the water and sugar together, and when cool, add to the rest. Then fit fermentation lock or cover as directed and continue to ferment in a warm place until all fermentation has ceased.

LEMON WINE

This wine is not ordinarily made to drink like wine. Experienced winemakers often make it for blending with dried fruit wines, which sometimes fall short of the acid requirement. But more often, it is made as a novelty. It is particularly suitable for making lemon gin wine. Use the above directions for making orange wine-using eight lemons instead of using oranges.

GRAPEFRUIT WINE

This is another acid wine, but many people like it, especially where a pound of raisins or dates are fermented with the grapefruits. Use eight large grapefruits following the orange wine recipe above. If you wish to add a pound of raisins or dates, do so as soon as you have cut up the grapefruits and ferment them with the rest for the first few days-until straining time.

NOTE: If raisins or dates are used, use half a pound less of sugar, because dried fruits contain approximately fifty percent sugar.

Flower Wines and Miscellaneous Recipes:

Flower wines, cannot, of course, be likened to any other homemade wine-or commercial wine-because their flavors are unique; they can only be described as delicately aromatic, their bouquet cannot be found in any other wine.

Their popularity is lessened only by the labor of collecting the flowers, but by choosing a spot where they abound, enough for a gallon or two may be gathered in an hour.

Care is needed if we are to get the best from our ingredients. When gathering the flowers, it is best to use a basket of ample size because crushing will damage the flowers, and we shall not get such a delightful wine. All flowers should be gathered on a dry day but not necessarily on a sunny one, though it must be sunny when collecting dandelions; otherwise, they are either closed or half-closed and difficult to find. In their closed state, they teem with insects that would get into the wine and spoil it. Dandelions close when gathered, but this

234 | MASTER WINEMAKING

does not matter. It is a great help because we should use only the petals of dandelions, and when they are closed, the petals may be pulled out all together merely by holding the head of the flower and pulling on the petals.

Although only petals should be used, many people make quite good dandelion wine by using the whole heads, but I use petals only.

A wine yeast should be used, and this may be an all-purpose wine yeast. Invert sugar should not be used in these recipes because it is inclined to slightly alter the aroma of the flower and change the delicate color of the wines made from recipes in this Lesson.

Bakers' yeast is included in the recipe together with household sugar; those preferring to use a wine yeast 'stated' as directed may, of course, do so.

GORSE WINE

5 pts. gorse flowers, 3 lb. sugar, 1 gal. water, 1 oz. yeast, Five pints is the minimum amount of gorse flowers to use, you may use more if you wish-up to one gallon if you can get them. Other ingredients would remain the same.

Put the flowers in the fermenting vessel and pour on half a gallon of boiling water. Cover and leave to soak for three days, stirring each day and covering again at once.

Boil half the sugar in a quart of water for two minutes, and when this is cool, add the flower mixture. Then add the yeast and ferment for three days. Strain out the flowers and continue to ferment the liquor in the fermenting vessel for a further seven days. Then pour into a gallon jar, leaving as much of the deposit behind as you can. Boil the rest of the sugar in the remaining water for two minutes, and when cool, add to the rest. Cover as directed or fit fermentation lock and continue to ferment until all fermentation has ceased.

NOTE: Many people prefer this when the juice of one lemon is added at the same time as the yeast.

CLOVER WINE

3 qts. clover heads, 2 lemons, 3 lb. sugar, 1 gal. water, 1 oz. yeast.

Pull off the petals by gathering them between the fingers while holding the base of the flower head. Put the petals in the fermenting vessel and pour on half a gallon of boiling water. Leave well covered for twelve hours. Boil half the sugar in a quart of water for two minutes, and when cool, add this to the rest. Then add the yeast and ferment the mixture for seven days.

Strain our the flowers, but do not squeeze too hard, and put the liquor into a gallon jar. Then boil the rest of the sugar in the remaining water, and when cool, add this to the rest. Cover or fit fermentation lock and leave until all fermentation has ceased.

DANDELION WINE

1 gal. flower heads with the tiniest piece of stalk, 3lb. sugar, 1 oz. yeast, 1 gal. water, 2 lemons.

Remove petals as directed for clover wine. Put the petals in the fermenting vessel and pour on three quarts of water-boiling and leave to soak for seven days, well covered.

Stir daily, and cover again at once. Stain and wring out fairly tightly and return the liquor to the fermenting vessel. Boil half the sugar in a pint of water and when cool add to the liquor, then add the yeast and the juice of two lemons. Cover as directed and ferment for seven days. Then pour carefully into a gallon jar, leaving as much deposit behind as you can. After this, boil the rest of the sugar in the remaining pint of water and, when cool, add to the rest.

Cover as directed or fit fermentation lock and leave until all fermentation has ceased.

COLTSFOOT WINE

1 gal. coltsfoot flower, 3 lb. sugar, 1 gal. water, 1 oz. yeast.

Pull the petals off in the same way as for dandelions. The method for making this wine is identical to the recipe for making dandelion wine.

HAWTHORN BLOSSOM WINE

2 qts. of the flower, 3 1/2 lb. sugar, 1 oz. yeast and 1 gal. water.

Gathered when they are about to drop, they may be shaken off into the fermenting vessel. The method for making this wine is identical to the recipe for making dandelion wine.

ELDERFLOWER WINE

1 gal. flower, 1 gal. water, 3 1/2 lb. sugar, 1 oz. yeast, 2 lemons.

Boil half the sugar in half a gallon of water and while boiling pour over the flowers in the fermenting vessel. Add the juice of the lemons, and when the mixture is cool, add the yeast. Cover as directed and ferment for seven days.

Strain out the flowers and wring out well, but not too dry. Put the strained liquor in a gallon jar. Boil the rest of the sugar and water for two minutes, and when cool, add to the rest. Cover as directed or fit fermentation lock and leave until all fermentation has ceased.

Another very good elderflower wine may be made in the same way as the above using only five pints of the flowers with three pounds of sugar, two lemons, 1 oz. yeast and one gallon of water.

ROSE PETAL WINE

This is one of the most delightful of all flower wines. The petals of roses of various colors may be used in a lot of wine, but if you have enough of, say, both red and yellow for a separate lot of each, do keep them separate.

3 qts. rose petals (strongly scented if possible), 1 gal. water, 3 lb. sugar, 1 oz. yeast, 2 lemons.

Pour half a gallon of boiling water over the petals in the fermenting vessel, cover well, and leave for forty-eight hours, stirring often.

Boil half the sugar in a quart of water for two minutes, and when this is cool, add to the petal mixture and ferment for three days. Strain and wring out well, and return the liquor to the fermenting vessel and let it ferment for a further ten days.

Pour the liquor into a gallon jar, leaving as much of the deposit behind as you can. Then boil the rest of the sugar and water as before and when cool, add to the rest together with the juice of the lemons. Cover again as directed or fit fermentation lock and leave until all fermentation has ceased.

TEA WINE

Many wine-makers save left-overs from the teapot until they have enough to make a gallon of wine, but I find that the flavor of the wine is somewhat impaired when this is done. Better to make a gallon of weak tea and to start straight off. Don't be tempted to make strong tea for this purpose; otherwise, you will have too much tannin in the wine.

8 teaspoons of tea, 1 gal. water, 1 lb. raisins, juice of 2 lemons, 3 lb. sugar, 1 oz. yeast.

Make tea in the usual way using eight teaspoonfuls and a quart of water. Let it stand undisturbed for ten minutes, and then strain into the fermenting vessel.

Boil half the sugar in half a gallon of water for two minutes, and when cool, add this to the tea. Then add the raisins and finely sliced lemons and their juice. Add the yeast and ferment for ten days, stirring daily.

Strain into a gallon jar. Then boil the rest of the sugar in the remainder of the water for two minutes, and when cool, add this to the rest. Cover as directed or fit fermentation lock and leave to ferment in a warm place until all fermentation has ceased.

IMITATION TIA MARIA

The best plan is to make either easy potato wine or easy parsnip wine, and when this has ceased fermenting flavor it with freshly made coffee. But do this very carefully as it is easy to overdo it, thus spoiling the flavor.

ROSEHIP WINE

Rose hips abound in early autumn, and it matters not whether they are gathered from your rose trees or the hedgerows. They should not be used until they have taken on their winter coat or red or orange according to the type.

4 lb. rose hips, 3 lb. sugar, 1 gal. water, 1 oz. yeast.

Wash the hips well in half a gallon of water in which one Campden tablet has been dissolved. Crush the hips with a mallet or chop them. Put them in the fermenting vessel and pour on half a gallon of boiling water. Boil half the sugar in a quart of water for two minutes, and when cooled, add a little to the rest. Add the yeast and ferment the pulp for seven days. Then strain out the solids and put the strained liquor into a gallon jar. Boil the rest of the sugar in the remaining water for two minutes and allow it to cool well before adding to the rest. Cover as directed or fit fermentation lock and leave to ferment in a warm place until all fermentation has ceased.

Wines From Dried Herbs:

In case the advantages of making wines from dried herbs do not immediately become evident, let me explain that the town and city dweller (and countryman, too, for that matter) may make all the old favorite wines of Granny's day for next to nothing. Practically no work is involved because, unlike fresh fruits which have to be gathered and roots that have to be scrubbed, grated and boiled, suitable packets of herbs are available ready to use. In cases, many town and city dwellers might well know of the old country wines and wish that they could make them- indeed, they may well have lived in the country and tasted the wines made from the fresh herbs; dandelion, sage, coltsfoot, mint, balm, yarrow, and countless others.

The actual amount of the dried article may be varied according to personal tastes, but usually, two ounces is enough for one gallon, and this amount rarely costs very much.

Those who know their herbs well enough to gather them fresh from the garden or field or hedgerow may do so, of course, but it must be borne in mind that one needs at least one pound of the fresh plant to get the equivalent of two ounces of the dried. It is most important one should be an expert at identification because many health-giving herbs bear a striking resemblance to others, which have proved themselves to be deadly poisonous.

In some of the recipes which follow the addition of raisins or wheat, or both, are recommended. At the same time, I would stress that their use is quite optional, I do strongly advise readers to use them where they are specified unless they know in advance that they prefer wines made without them. The use of raisins or wheat, or both, adds body and bouquet where these properties may be lacking. As you will have guessed, the herb gives only flavor-apart from its known medicinal properties-and some aroma but does not give the same amount of bouquet as a fully flavored fruit; wheat and raisins help in this respect. As with root wines, the addition of acid is necessary, and this way may be added as citric acid at the rate of a quarter-ounce per gallon or as the juice of two large lemons-whichever suits you best.

The amounts of sugar in the recipes are those generally used, but readers now know that they make their herb wines dry merely by reducing the amount of sugar according to their wishes.

It should be borne in mind that while we use a gallon of water, and while the sugar, occupies space at the rate of a quart to every four pounds, we shall arrive back at the gallon of wine aimed at because there will be some loss during boiling, lost of most of the sugar which will be fermented out and some small wastage when transferring to other bottles. A little less sugar is used in these recipes as compared with fresh fruit wines; this is because there is no acidity or astringency to balance, as is often the case where fruit wines are made.

When fermentation has nearly ceased, you may sample for the strength of flavor; if you feel you would like it stronger, a little more of the herb may be added, but this should not be necessary. On the other hand, if the flavor happens to be a little too strong, a pint or two or boiled and cooled water may be added to dilute the strength or flavor. It will increase the overall amount of wine so that the amount of sugar added will not be enough for the increased amount. Therefore, when boiling the additional water, with it three to four ounces of sugar to each pint and then add this syrup slowly, taking samples until the strength of flavor is right.

Where Kola nuts are used, a ten packet is enough.

All dried herbs may be obtained from most chemists, but sometimes their stock is likely to be a little old. Health and Heather deal in this field to such a large extent that their herbs can be relied upon to give the best results. Alternatively, get them from a reliable herbalist if you have one in your locality.

The following method is suitable for all recipes in this Lesson.

Lemons and oranges should be peeled, the fruit broken up and added, and the peel discarded.

METHOD: Put all the ingredients (except sugar and yeast) in a polythene pail and pour on half a gallon of boiling water, leave for two or three hours covered as directed. Then boil half the sugar in a quart of water or two minutes and add this to the rest while still boiling. Mix well, and when cool enough, add the yeast and nutrient. Cover again and ferment in a pail in a warm place for ten days, stirring daily and covering again at once.

After ten days, strain out the solids and wring out as dry as you can, and put the strained liquor into a gallon glass bottle. Boil the other half of the sugar in the remaining quart of water for two minutes, and when cool, add this to the rest. Cover as directed or fit with a fermentation lock and continue to ferment in a warm place until all fermentation has ceased.

BALM WINE

2 oz. dried balm leaves, 2 lemons, 3 lb. sugar, 1 gal. water, yeast, and nutrient.

PARSLEY WINE

2 oz. dried parsley, 1 oz. dried mint, (or 1/2 oz., fresh mint), 1/2 oz. dried sage (red), 1 gal. water, 2 oranges, 2 lemons, 3 lb. sugar, (or 3 3/4 lb. invert), yeast and nutrient.

BROOM WINE

2 oz. dried broom flowers, 2 lemons, 1 lb. raisins, 2 ½ lb. sugar (or 3 1/4 lb. invert), yeast and nutrient.

DAMIKOLA WINE

2 oz. dried damiana leaves, 1 oz. kola nuts, 1/2 oz. dried red sage, 1 lb. raisins, 3 lb. sugar (or 3 3/4 lb. invert), 2 lemons, 1 gal. water, yeast, and nutrient.

SAGE WINE

3 oz. dried sage, 1 lb. raisins, 1 oz. dried mint, 1 lb. wheat, 2 lemons, 2 1/2 lb. sugar (or 3 1/4 lb. invert), yeast and nutrient, 1 gal. water.

YARROW WINE

2 to 3 oz. of dried yarrow flowers, 2 lemons, 2 oranges, 3 lb. sugar (or 3 3/4 lb. invert), 1 gal. water, yeast nutrient.

CLARY WINE

3 to 4 oz. clary flowers, 1 lb. raisins, 2 lemons, 3 lb. sugar (or 3 3/4 lb. invert), 1 gal. water, yeast, and nutrient.

BURNET WINE

3 oz. burnet herb, 1 lb. raisins, 1 lb. wheat, 2 oranges, 2 lemons, 3 lb. sugar (or 3 3/4 lb. invert), 1 gal. water, yeast, and nutrient.

It is strongly advised that you experiment with half-gallon lots of these and to add tiny amounts of aniseed or licorice as fermentation nears completion. If you do this with varying amounts of herbs, you must not let the total weight of the herbs exceed four ounces to the gallon of wine being made. I realize, of course, that a beginner cannot have any definite plan for blending because he will not be familiar with the flavors given to the wines by the various herbs. If you accidentally spoil the flavor of a wine by trying to improve it, you may dilute with sugar-water, and while fermentation is still going on, add other herbs to the flavor you are aiming at. If you happen to find that the flavor is not quite strong enough, you may suspend a bag of herbs in the fermenting 'must' until you get the strength of flavor you want. And this may be tested at few-day intervals by tasting.

No matter how many years you may have been making wines and no matter how many different varieties you have made, it will be clear from the number of recipes in this book that there is plenty you have not tried your hand at. However, do not be tempted to make thirty or forty different varieties on a grand scale. Make, say, half a dozen build lots with recipes and fruit you are familiar with and experiment with half-gallon lots. In this way, you will always have a nice stock, and if any particular experiment goes wrong or perhaps does not turn out quite as hoped, little will be lost.

Wines From Dried Fruits and Grain:

The making of wines from grain and dried fruits is a boom to the townsman who finds these ingredients easily obtainable, and they make good wines. Mixtures of dried fruit and grains make for strong, fully flavored, but not too fully flavored wines which, when not made too sweet, are often likened to whiskeys and brandies. They need time to mature or reach their best-two years is not too long, though at one year old they are very excellent wines. As with root wines, the addition of some acid is necessary here (see root wines), and this is put into the 'must' in the form of oranges and lemons.

Most dried fruit is heavily sulphited to prevent fermentation, and most wheat or other grain has been in contact with all sorts of dirt, dust, and bacteria. Therefore they must be well cleaned before use.

Break up the raisins and drop them into boiling water. As soon as the water boils again, cut off the heat, strain the raisins, and throw the water away. The raisins are then ready to use. Do the same with wheat or other grain, but use a separate saucepan; they are then ready to use.

A WORD ABOUT TANNIN

Most recipes for fruit wines allow for tannin in the fruits to be given into the 'must.' This tannin forms an important part of the flavor of the wine-though few people realize it. But they soon know when there is too much because the wine takes on the flavor or 'tang' of strong unsweetened tea. The little tannin given to fruit wines is usually just the right amount.

Ordinarily, there is no tannin present in dried fruit wines. Therefore it is as well to add one tablespoonful of freshly made tea-not too strong-to make good this deficiency. Special grape tannin is available, but tea is a cheap and handy source of which we might as well make use. The addition of tea is included in the recipes.

RAISIN WINE

3 lb. raisins, 3 lemons, 2 lb. sugar, 9 pts. water, 1 oz. yeast, 1 tablespoonful of freshly made tea.

Less sugar than usual is required here because the large number of raisins will give a lot of sugar to the wine - which will not be dry. For a dry raisin, wine use only one and a quarter pound of sugar. Put the raisins and the sliced lemons and the tea in the Fermenting vessel. Boil all the sugar in all the water (or half the water at a time if your saucepan is on the small side), and add the rest while boiling. When cool, add the yeast and ferment for fourteen days, stirring daily and covering again at once. Strain and wring out as dry as you can and put the strained liquor into a gallon jar. Cover as directed or fit fermentation lock and leave until all fermentation has ceased.

PRUNE PORT

6 lb. prunes, 2 lemons, 3 1/2 lb. sugar, 9 pts. water, 1oz. yeast. (no tea in this one.)

Wash the prunes in water in which one Campden tablet has been dissolved and put them in the fermenting vessel. Boil two pounds sugar in seven pints of water and pour over the fruit while boiling. Allow to cool and add the yeast. Cover and ferment for ten days, crushing well each day as soon as the fruit has become soft and then after ten days, crush well and strain out the solids. Wring out as dry as you can and put the strained liquor in a gallon jar. Boil the rest of the sugar in the remaining two pints of water, and when cool, add the rest. Cover as directed or fit fermentation lock and leave until all fermentation has ceased.

CURRANT WINE

No lemons are required here as currants contain sufficient acid, neither is tea required.

4 lb. currants, 1 lb. raisins, 2 3/4 lb. sugar, 1 oz. yeast, 9 pts. water.

Prepare the currants by the method given for prunes in the previous recipe, and put in the fermenting vessel. Boil half the sugar (or roughly half) in seven pints water for two minutes and pour on to the currants at once. Allow to cool and add the yeast. Cover as directed and ferment for twelve days, crushing and covering again each day.

After twelve days, strain out the solids and wring out as dry as you can and put the strained liquor into a gallon jar.

Boil the rest of the sugar in the remaining two pints of water for two minutes, and when cool, add to the rest. Cover as directed or fit fermentation lock and leave until all fermentation has ceased.

DRIED APRICOT WINE

6 lb. dried apricots, w oranges, 3 1/2 lb. sugar, 9 pts. water, 1 oz. yeast, 1 tablespoonful of freshly made tea.

Put the apricots in the fermenting vessel with the cut-up oranges and their peel. Fold the orange peel and squeeze to get as much oil out of it as you can.

Boil two pounds of sugar in seven pints of water for two minutes and pour over the fruits while still boiling. Allow to cool and add the yeast. Cover as directed and ferment for ten days, crushing by hand each day and covering again at once.

After ten days, strain and wring out as dry as you can an put the strained liquor in the gallon jar. Boil the remaining sugar in the last two pints of water for two minutes and when cool, add to the rest and then add the tea. Cover as directed or fit fermentation lock and leave until all fermentation has ceased.

DATE WINE

This wine has very little flavor of its own; therefore, lemons and oranges must be added to give a nice flavor, and the number of oranges here will make it into a lovely wine.

However, if you want a wine of little flavor for some special purpose, say, blending with one that has too much flavor or for flavoring as you wish with an extract or whatever you may have in mind, use no oranges at all.

3 lb. of packeted or loose dates, 1 lemon, 6 oranges, 2 lb. sugar, 9 pts. water, 1 oz. yeast 1 tablespoonful of freshly made tea.

The method of preparing ingredients and making this wine is identical to that given in the recipe for making dried apricot wine.

PRUNE AND RAISIN VINTAGE

3 lb. prunes, 1 lb. raisins, 1 lb. wheat, 2 lemons, 2 oranges, 3 lb. sugar, 9 pts. water, 1 oz. yeast.

Prepare the raisins, prunes, and wheat as has already been advised and put them with the sliced oranges and lemons in the fermenting vessel. Boil half the sugar in seven pints water for two minutes and pour over the ingredients while still boiling. Allow to cool and add the yeast. Cover as directed and ferment the mixture for ten days, crushing well each day and stirring up the wheat and covering again at once. After ten days, strain out the solids, and wring out as dry as you can and put the strained liquor in a gallon jar. Boil the rest of the sugar in the remaining two pints of water, and when cool, add to the rest. Cover as directed or fit fermentation lock and leave until all fermentation has ceased.

LIQUEURS

One bottle of gin, whiskey, or brandy will give you two bottles of the finished product with a high percentage of alcohol to half the cost of the commercial product.

Before going on to the recipes, let's explain that a homemade wine usually has an alcohol content of fourteen percent by volume (approximately 24 proof). Such a wine will keep well because this amount of alcohol is usually high enough to destroy souring yeast and the bacteria, which causes "vinegariness" immediately when it comes in contact with them. Thus it will be seen that a nice percentage of alcohol acts as its preservative.

The alcohol content of commercial wines rarely exceeds twenty percent by volume (approximately 35 proof); more often, they range between fourteen percent by volume (approximately 24 proof) and nineteen percent (approximately 33 proof), which is a high percentage of alcohol. We could very well dilute the 70 proof gin (forty percent by volume) to 35 proof (twenty percent by volume) by making one bottle into two bottles and still have a very strong sloe gin. Whiskey and rum could be similarly treated, while brandy might well be diluted even more owing to its higher spirit content. Bear in mind that it would be unwise to reduce the proof to below 30. The best plan to start with is to make one bottle into two as the recipes advise or make half a bottle into a whole bottle by using half of everything in the recipes.

You could make three or four bottles from one bottle of the spirit if you were proposing to use it up fairly quickly, such as at a party or over the three day Christmas.

Naturally, we shall be diluting the flavors of the spirits we are using, but we shall be adding the flavors of our choice to counter-balance this. In any case, the commercial spirits mentioned above are rarely drunk neat. Whiskey is usually diluted with water or ginger ale, while rum is often diluted with cola. Gin is usually diluted with tonic.

Therefore, the proof spirit content of the whiskey and soda or gin and tonic served over the bar has been reduced to about 23 proof. The sloe gin we shall be made with these recipes will be 35 proof, while the cherry brandy will be 40 proof. Bear this in mind while drinking them; otherwise, you will finish up under the table in double-quick time.

If you happen to have some home-made sloe wine, damson wine, orange wine, cherry wine, or some other sort of home-made wine, you may employ one bottle of the spirits to make more than two bottles of cherry brandy, sloe gin or whichever you have in mind. This point is covered fully further on in this lesson.

The following recipes produce wines that are neither sweet nor dry; if you like a slightly sweet wine, increase the amount of sugar by half that given in the recipes. On the other hand, if you like wines drier than average, reduce the amount of sugar by half.

In the recipes called liqueurs, the amount of sugar should remain as in the recipes.

NOTE: As we shall be using bottles as our means of measuring our materials, bear in mind that a bottle is a bottle, and half a bottle is half a bottle. A bottle - the recognized standard wine bottle or the bottles containing spirits-hold five gills; this is one gill more than a pint. Many bottles containing imported wines hold one pint. Because we shall be making exactly two bottles from one bottle of the spirit we are using, be sure to at the second bottle you use holds the same amount as the bottle of spirit you are using.

CHERRY BRANDY LIQUEUR

1 1/2 lb. black cherries, 8 oz. white sugar, 1 bottle brandy, 8 blanched almonds (these are usually added, but personal tastes must decide.)

Wash the cherries and let the drain. Pour the brandy into a four-pound Kilner jar (these are best), then stone and halve the cherries carefully and add them to the brandy. Add the almonds if you like them.

Screw down tightly and put in a cool, preferably dark place for six to eight weeks. Give the jar a good shaking twice a week. Strain and squeeze and put the liquid into a smaller jar, then put away as before and leave to clear. Then pour or siphon into two wine bottles-putting exactly half into each. Then boil the sugar in one pint of water for two minutes. When this is cool, fill the bottles to within one inch of where the cork will reach. Shake well to ensure thorough mixing. Seal and keep for one month.

DAMSON GIN

1 lb. damsons, 3 oz. sugar, 1 bottle gin.

Wash, dry, stone, and halve the damsons carefully and put them in a four-pound Kilner jar. Sprinkle the sugar over them and then pour in the gin. Screw down tightly and leave in a cool dark place for three months (or two months if you are in a hurry to use the product), giving a good shaking once or twice a week.

Strain and squeeze and put the strained damson gin into a smaller jar, screw-down again, and put it away to clear. Then pour carefully (or siphon) the clear gin off the deposit, putting exactly half into two bottles. Then fill the bottles to within one inch of where the corks will reach with boiled water that has cooled naturally. Cork and keep for one month.

SLOE GIN

1 lb. sloes, 5 oz. sugar, 1 bottle gin.

Wash the sloes and let them drain. Prick the sloes all over with a silver, or stainless-steel fork or large darning needle and put them in a four-pound Kilner jar. Sprinkle the sugar over them and then pour in the gin. Screw down tightly and put in a cool dark place for six weeks. Give the jar a good shaking once a week.

Strain and squeeze and put the strained sloe gin into a smaller jar, screw-down tightly again, and put away until clear. Pour carefully (or siphon) the clear sloe gin off the deposit and put exactly half into each of two bottles. Fill the bottles to within one inch of where the corks will reach with boiled water that has cooled naturally. Mix well by shaking, cork seal, and keep for one month.

ORANGE WHISKY

4 oranges, 2 lemons, 2 Seville oranges (or an extraordinary orange and lemon), 4 oz. sugar, 1 bottle whiskey.

Peel the fruits and remove all the white pith. Crush well and put the pulp in a four pound Kilner jar. Grate the rind of one orange (not a Seville), avoiding any white pith, and add this to the pulp. Sprinkle in the sugar and pour on the whiskey. Screw down tightly and put the jar in a cool dark place for a week-giving it a shake every day.

Strain into another jar and squeeze the screw-down again tightly, then put it away to clear. Pour or siphon the clear whiskey into bottles, putting exactly half into each. Then fill the bottles to within an inch of where the corks will reach with boiled water that has cooled naturally. Cork hark, seal, and keep for at least two months.

ORANGE GIN

6 oranges, 1 lemon, 2 Seville oranges (or an extraordinary orange and lemon), 5 oz. sugar, 1 bottle gin.

Proceed as for orange whiskey.

Fruit Liqueurs:

There is no need to give separate recipes for each fruit because the same process may be used for all suitable fresh fruit of your choice.

The following lists the most suitable fruits for liqueur-making, and the amounts given usually produce sufficient flavor-though not enough juice-to make two bottles of liqueur when using one bottle of brandy. If not enough juice is produced from the amounts of fruit given, make up the amount required with boiled water, bearing in mind that half a pound of sugar occupies the space of a quarter-pint while one pound occupies half a pint space and so on. All these liqueurs will have a spirit content of 40proof-which, as we have seen, is a high spirit content.

As we shall be using a spirit of 80 proof, we could make two and a half bottles by using a little more juice, a little more water, and an ounce or two more sugar and still have a product of 32 proof-which is a nice spirit content.

If at party time economy is essential, three or even four bottles of a liqueur-type wine could be made from one bottle of brandy or, say, cherry brandy, sloe gin or whatever you have in mind if it were intended to use them up over a weekend or over a three day Christmas.

See making liqueurs from wines and making liqueurs from extracts.

One bottle of liqueur may be made by using exactly half the amounts listed below and a little water.

Fresh Fruit	Quantity (lb.)	Sugar (oz.)	Brandy
Black currants	1	4	1 bottle
Red currants	1.5	5	1 bottle
Strawberries	1.5	3	1 bottle
Cherries	2	4	1 bottle
Raspberries	1	5	1 bottle
Loganberries	1	4	1 bottle
Blackberries	1	5	1 bottle

Crush the fruit by hand, put in a basin, and keep in a very warm place for twelve hours, well covered. Strain carefully through several thicknesses of fine muslin or other suitable material. Allow to drain rather than squeeze.

Put the strained juice into a bottle of the same size as the brandy bottle and fill with boiled water that has been allowed to cool. Mix well by shaking, cork hard, and put in a cool place for one hour. By this time, a deposit will have formed. Pour the clear juice off this deposit, leaving a little juice rather than allowing any deposit through. The deposit may cause permanent cloudiness if boiled with the clear juice.

Put the clear juice in a small unchipped enamel saucepan with the sugar and boil gently for two minutes. When cool, put exactly half into two bottles of the same size as the brandy bottle and then fill up with brandy. Add a few drops of boiled water if the liquid does not reach to within one inch of where the corks will reach. Then cork and seal after giving a good shaking to ensure thorough mixing and keep for at least a month. If a film of deposit forms at the bottom of the bottles decant before serving.

Liqueurs and Party Specials (from home-made wines):

Most of us have stocks of home-made wine, and at party time or Christmas, we often wonder how we can turn them into 'party specials' and do so inexpensively. The main question always is how many spirits to add to get a given percentage of alcohol.

A well-made wine will not need doctoring because if fermentation were satisfactory, the alcohol content would be in the region of fourteen percent by volume (24 to 26 proof). This is the alcohol content of most commercial wines; indeed, some are lower in alcohol than this while others are, of course, higher.

Come party time the question is often one of economy-how to make that one bottle of Scotch, or gin or rum, go farther without the economy being noticeable. For those who want to experiment a bit on their own accord, the table shows the relation between alcohol by volume and proof spirit, and the range covered by this allows for the limits within which they will be working. Those not wishing to start from scratch will find the following guide useful.

Let me begin with whiskey, gin, or rum of 70 proof. Wines made with the following fruits are ideal for mixing with gin, either sweetened or unsweetened-damson, sloe, lemon, orange.

We have a bottle of one or the other of these wines and a bottle of gin handy. The gin contains forty percent alcohol by volume and a bottle of wine fourteen percent. Mix the two, and you have (for the sake of simplicity) twice as much of both. Therefore you have twenty percent by volume (the gin), and seven percent by volume (the wine), a total of twenty-seven percent by volume.

To make it simpler:

- The gin 40 percent by volume
- The wine 14 percent by volume
- 54 percent

But because the volume (amount) has been doubled, the alcohol content has been reduced by half-twenty seven percent by volume. As we can get fifty-four percent of alcohol in this way, we could use two bottles of wine and one of gin and get three bottles of a product containing eighteen percent.

NOTE: It is important to understand that when two bottles of wine at 14% of alcohol are put together, you have twice as much wine still at 14%. But when you do this to fortify, the alcohol in each bottle must be accounted for. Therefore, three bottles of wine, each containing 14%, equals 42%, plus one bottle of gin at 40% = 82%. Divide this figure by the number of resulting bottles, in this case, four bottles-and each will contain just over 20%.

Going further: 5 bottles at 14% = 70%

1 bottle gin at 40%

Total of 110%

In this case, six bottles result, therefore 110 divided by 6 = 18% approximately. The same would apply when whiskey or rum is used.

Wines more suitable for mixing with whiskey are Root wines (not beetroot). Root wines made with cereals such as wheat, and with raisins, or both, or with wheat or raisins alone added. Grain wines -- those made mainly with wheat or maize, etc. Orange. Dandelion.

Wines more suitable for mixing with rum:

- Root wines with a rather higher than average acid content.
- Other more acidic wines such as rhubarb.
- Orange.
- Lemon.
- Grapefruit.

Wines more suitable for mixing with port and other high alcohol red wines:

- Elderberry
- All of the red wines (whether made from one fruit or a mixture of fruits, or mixtures of fruits and grains such as wheat or maize)
- White wines
- Paler-color ones made from such fruits as raisins,

raspberries, loganberries, red or white currants, etc., may be mixed with the higher-alcohol white 'ports' or high-alcohol white wines.

NOTE: Owing to the lower alcohol content of port as compared with spirits, the mixing should be confined to one bottle of wine to the bottle of port if they are required for keeping. Two to one mixing may be practiced where it is intended to use up the product within, say, three or four days.

INVERT SUGAR

It can be made at home if you have difficulty obtaining some: Put 8 lb. of ordinary household sugar (white sugar) in a suitable pan with 2 pints of water and 1/2 ounce of citric acid (obtainable at a wine-making store), or use the juice of four lemons. Bring slowly to a boil, stirring all the time so that all sugar dissolves.

When all sugar is dissolved, allow to boil for half an hour very gently without stirring or stirring only occasionally. Allow this to cool some-what and then makeup to exactly 1 gallon by adding boiled water.

You now have INVERT SUGAR - the inversion being caused by the acid. To measure, use 1 pint to each lb. sugar called for in the recipe - 1 pint is equal to 1 lb. sugar. Store in suitable jars, tightly corked.

YEAST NUTRIENTS

These are blends of chemicals that stimulate yeast reproduction, thereby helping the yeast to make as much alcohol as it is capable of making. There are no real substitutes.

CAMPDEN TABLETS

Four grains of sodium metabisulfite is equivalent to one Campden tablet. You can get metabisulfite or Campden tablets at any wine-making store.

RIBENA

If you cannot obtain this, try to substitute black-currant syrup instead. However, it is best to use RIBENA proper.

Made in the USA
Monee, IL
24 May 2021

69342459R00144